REAL
ESTATE
PROSPECTING

REAL ESTATE PROSPECTING

TRISTAN AHUMADA

Create a Million-Dollar Life
Through Relationships, Online Leads,
Technology, and Social Media

WILEY

Published by John Wiley & Sons, Inc., Hoboken, New Jersey.
Published simultaneously in Canada.

For general information on our other products and services or for technical support, please contact our Customer Care Department within the United States at (800) 762-2974, outside the United States at (317) 572-3993 or fax (317) 572-4002.

Wiley also publishes its books in a variety of electronic formats. Some content that appears in print may not be available in electronic formats. For more information about Wiley products, visit our web site at www.wiley.com.

Library of Congress Cataloging-in-Publication Data is Available:

ISBN 9781394172160 (cloth)
ISBN 9781394172177 (ePub)
ISBN 9781394172184 (ePDF)

Cover Design: Wiley
Cover Images: © Fox Design/Shutterstock

SKY10044057_030723

To Janice, Aliyah, and Ansen.
I do this all for you.

Contents

Contents

Acknowledgments

I would like to thank the following people for their help in creating this book:

My mom and dad. . .you know who you are. You made me into who I am.

Traci Hohenstein, couldn't have done this one without your consistent help!

My awesome friends and staff at A Brilliant Tribe and Lab Coat Agents.

Chris Smith, who introduced me to Wiley Publishing!

Jeff Pfitzer, my friend who nudges me about everything I forget to do.

Nick Baldwin, my Lab Coat Agents friend and business partner.

My long time Real Estate team, Mayra Zuniga, Cathy Waters, Valerie Sundareswaran, Luis Robledo, John Chowdhury, Mark Rader, Zack Neeley, Jacob Steagall, Tiffany Canare, Jacob Frye, and I know I missed about 20 more of you. . .

For their contributions to the book: Hoss Pratt, Darryl Davis, Leisel and Donnell Taylor, and Justin Havre.

All the nice folks at Wiley Publishing, especially Richard, Debbie, Jessica, and Rene.

My editor, Lori Martinsek and her team.

And anyone else I may have forgotten—my sincere apologies. I promise to mention you in the next book!

The Fundamentals

Chapter 1

Attract More Business

In 2013, I was traveling by plane from Los Angeles to San Francisco. Although it wasn't a long journey, it was our family's first time flying. I had just accepted an invitation from Realtor.com to address a group of more than 10,000 real estate agents. A few thousand agents in the US and Canada were already using my systems and processes for converting online leads, and Realtor.com wanted me to show them all how to do it more effectively.

I glanced over at Janice, my wife, during the flight and leaned in to say, "Hey, this is all cool, but I'm not sure if this will be a one-time thing or if this will last. What do you think we should do with this opportunity?"

Janice replied, "I don't know, but what are you thinking?"

I quickly said, "I'm thinking of creating a blog. A place that I can write about how we convert online leads, with all the tech we use and the systems we have."

I was inspired by a real estate blog that had been popular at the time. It was called *Tech Savvy Agent*, and it was run by two of my friends, Chris Smith and Steve Pacinnelli.

What Janice said next challenged me, and it's one of the main reasons we make the best team. "I don't think so," she said. "Why don't you try creating a Facebook group? That could be great."

I gave it a serious thought for a while, but then I quickly rejected the notion. In actuality, it took me until October 2, 2014—nearly a year later—to launch the Facebook group that served as the catalyst for the entire movement.

The lesson here is to always check to see where the bigger opportunity is with what's trending. The saying by Wayne Gretzy, "Skate to where the puck is going, not where it has been," has some merit.

When I first started Lab Coat Agents, I had no idea it would grow to be the world's largest online real estate agent community. I created it to assist real estate agents all over the world in boosting their bottom line through technology, processes, tools, and systems, as well as by providing advice that isn't out of date.

Here we are again. Although the world is changing quickly, most people still use antiquated methods of communication and collaboration with clients. While there is nothing wrong with doing some things the old-fashioned way, the key to progress is to do those things using modern technology. I want you to start thinking about attracting business instead of just hunting for it.

The majority of you are familiar with the meaning of prospecting. It's a phrase that describes what gold miners would do to find gold and is used in sales, mainly real estate. Most people associate the word negatively, so I want to change the image that comes to mind when you think of prospecting. I want to give you the road map, the tools, and the exact things to do so when you think of prospecting, you think of it in a new way. Prospecting should really be called "attracting."

How are you going to go out and attract people to work with you today?

Instead of calling people and forcing them to talk to you by using an outdated script or going out every day to spam them, you are calling people to connect with them and help them. Because you offer value, people are drawn to you. This is the foundation of the prospecting I teach.

It's not you going out to work your ass off to find the next person to work with. It's you going out there to show those you connect with the value you have so they can choose to work with you.

You've heard the sales term, "Every day you start from zero." Well, not with what we do. Every day you need to show up, but you don't start from zero. You start with the number of people that already love you and show up for you. Your job is to show up for them and keep attracting more people to your brand.

The majority of people dislike this method of doing business because it actually requires a lot of time and effort to develop relationships. Growing your influence takes time. It takes time to approach situations with values-driven ideas. This is how you develop a genuine, long-lasting business—a business that you can look back at a few years from now and know that you are leaving a legacy rather than just another business that will die off when you step out.

Although it took me years to launch Lab Coat Agents, the impact I had on the sector by consistently providing value was enormous. We encountered some incredible people along the way. In fact, when my wife and I made the decision to turn Lab Coat Agents into a legitimate business, we teamed up with my friend Nick Baldwin and expanded it even further. Lab Coat Agents has allowed my wife and me to grow companies like A Brilliant Tribe and Drunk On Social (a special thank you to Jeff Pfitzer), and now I have multiple partners in and out of the real estate world.

I want you to attract more business.

This is where you start.

I call it "Real Estate Prospecting."

Chapter 2

Environment and Finding Your Strength

When you start in real estate, you find that most companies tell you what to do. They outline a set of things you need to do. They call it "real estate prospecting." This includes making a list of the people you know and calling them, doing open houses, door knocking, making cold calls, and other similar activities. This is, in fact, how I started. It was May 2004. I had just gotten my real estate license, and I had one month left to graduate from college. The day I received my license, I went door knocking.

I printed out some flyers and knocked for six hours straight. I quickly realized that door knocking and being dressed up in a suit with dress shoes was not going to work for me in the summer California weather. The next thing I was told to do was to pick up the phone and make cold calls to neighborhoods that I wanted to work in. I started in real estate in my early twenties, and most of the people I knew at that time were not looking to buy a house because they couldn't afford it yet. I had two things going for me though, my background was in telemarketing/sales, and my mom had a great database.

I worked hard, and I got lucky. Luck was on my side because I had practiced how to talk to people for years prior. Through high school and college, I was trained in selling ink cartridges, windows, and a few other telemarketing jobs that forced me to excel at tonality and dialogue. I know most agents I talk to don't have the training, and you don't need it. The mistake that is made most often is the brokerage.

The brokerage or team you go to will outline the activities you need to do to be successful in real estate without taking into consideration all that you are great at already. Most of the things you are told to do to succeed in real estate actually work, but they don't work the same for everyone. The missing factor is your strength.

What are you great at? Think about it. Take a moment to think about why people love being around you. Take a moment to think about what types of people gravitate toward you.

Do you find yourself at the gym often? Are you a runner? Do you love playing pickleball? Do you have a meetup group to play Dungeons and Dragons? Do you belong to student/parent groups? Do you have a reading group?

I need you to think deeper. You already have a set of skills that can be applied to real estate, but no one is helping you close that gap. What makes real estate different is you.

What about you?

My 11-year-old son needed some help outlining some great qualities of his so he could write a good persuasive paragraph for getting elected into student council.

I had him grab an index card to outline his great qualities, and that helped him complete the paragraph.

Have you taken the time to outline what you're amazing at?

When you focus on what you're great at, you gain momentum, you see quicker progress, and in most cases, you find a groove to grow into the next version of yourself.

In the words of Peter Drucker, one of the greatest business writers of the 20th century, "We need to know our strengths in order to know where we belong."

You are the key factor in the success or failure you will encounter in real estate. People will be attracted to working with you, not because you follow a specific set of scripts that were used in the 1980s. You won't succeed by showing up at open houses and hoping that people will want to work with you. It takes effort on your part to showcase your authenticity through the value you choose to give to the audience you want to attract.

What I'm about to tell you in the following sentences is the key to changing your life for the better, faster and in ways you have only dreamed about. I have to thank my wife, Janice, for this as well. I'm naturally an introvert, but she literally has to kick me out of the house to connect with people and go to events. If you know me well, you know how hard it is for me to leave my cave at home.

One thing that I've found to be an often unspoken truth, an actual law of life, is that *your beliefs will dictate your behavior*. When you think about it deeper, you will agree with that sentence, but I want to tell you how to begin to change your beliefs. It's not easy, and it starts with challenging how you look at life.

The greatest sales books always start with the mindset and how important it is. It's important to have a strong mind that focuses on opportunities, but before you can think about success, you need to be exposed to it. Let's talk about that exposure. This is how you begin to change what's possible and how you begin to think differently.

Consistently attending industry talks, events, and mastermind sessions with people doing things at a higher level than you are key. When you are able to see what is possible, you begin to believe that things can change. For me, it started with my first event that I ever attended, which was a Tony Robbins event in 2006. I saw what others were achieving, what was possible, and what I could do differently to grow. In 2009, I attended a huge Keller Williams event that helped me to think bigger.

I sat in the audience as I heard agents talk about what they were doing to succeed. There are countless different ways to succeed at such a high level. I remember being inspired, and more importantly, I believed it was possible for me to achieve greater success in real estate. I made a plan for the second phase of my real estate business. Up to that point, I had already had massive financial success in real estate, but I needed to see what else was possible. The key was talking to people who had done it already or ones that were currently achieving it. This was hard for me because I feel out of place in big rooms with a lot of people.

There's a second part to being exposed to awesomeness. It's not just in person, but you can do it with books, podcasts, webinars, and social media. Read books that can show you new ways of succeeding in real estate, listen to podcasts that can enlighten you about what's happening in real estate, and watch things that can keep your mental and real estate skills sharp.

This, above all other things, must be a priority in your life. Who you surround yourself with in this world will determine how you think, what you think about, and what you do with your thoughts. It's the determining factor to your success. It is what economists would call leading indicators in the financial world. If we apply this to your life, then the leading indicators to your success in life and in real estate will be how many quality events you attend, how often you talk to high achievers, and how much information you consume that pertains to real estate and bettering yourself. The consistency and combination of this will make you quite uncomfortable because it will change how you operate. It will change your beliefs, which will change how you think, and this will change your actions.

Success isn't only about achieving financial success. We have all seen people who are wealthy but hate their lives. It's about making sure that every day you show up for yourself, so that you are better this year than you were last year. How often you show up for yourself will determine your success in life. Let's talk about how to create this in your life.

Tech
Audible
Brilliant Talks podcast

Chapter 3

Your Routine Matters

The key to a great day begins the night before. When I realized this, I devised a system centered on planning your day. PREPARE and MARVEL are the acronyms for it. These two acronyms simplify your daily routines. It started as an experiment on myself that turned into research, conversations, and interviews, which then helped me create the two acronyms. I have a whole book about this routine, but I condensed it into a chapter so you can apply this to your life today.

PREPARE and MARVEL are the evening and morning routines that also include a set of questions that will make you mindful and aware of the important aspects of your life.

We will start with the **PREPARE** portion first.

The formula for PREPARE is easy to remember: **P**lan, **R**eview, **E**xercise, **P**ractice, **A**ffirmations, **R**eflect, and **E**mbrace. This method will enhance your nightly rituals while also raising your awareness of your thoughts and behaviors throughout the day. It will also include exercises to protect your abilities, skills, and ambitions from digital distractions and minor diversions, allowing your life to unfold from the inside out, changing how people interact with you.

The wonderful thing about routines is that we all have them. For the majority of us, it's something we ignore; we wake up and let the day unfold as we pick up our devices and get going. What I've noticed is that successful people are much more deliberate in their work. They organize their actions around what they consider to be important, and this becomes a habit. The idea of success differs from person to person, so those automatic routines gravitate toward different things depending on the person. Because not everyone is fortunate enough to have routines that lead to a more fruitful life and purposeful existence, I've taken the time to identify the critical components of these routines and break them down so you can incorporate them into your daily process.

PREPARE

It starts at any time you want it to begin in the evening, so you can transition into being present at home for yourself and, if you have a family, for your family.

> **P: Plan.** We all know we should do it, but not everyone takes the time to adequately plan for the next day. This is

when you spend a few minutes evaluating the events of the day and your priorities for the day ahead to ensure you don't forget anything important. Simple.

R: Review. Days fly by so quickly and we are bombarded with so much information that it is natural to overlook something. This is the time to review your tasks, priorities, notes, schedule, email, voicemail, and texts to determine if you missed anything that needs to be addressed the following day. This review phase is designed to function as a catch-all to ensure that no minor things are overlooked.

E: Exercise: This section can be a full-fledged exercise session for you, or you can do what I do. I do some push-ups and sit-ups for two or three minutes, but it does not replace my workout period. I do a full workout in the middle of the day, so this is just something I do at the end of the day to get the blood pumping. It's a fact that the mind is linked to the body, and motion creates emotion, so jump in and finish it!

P: Practice gratitude: This might vary greatly from person to person. The cycle is completed by ending the day with time to reflect on what you are grateful for. It sets the tone for a day filled with gratitude for the people in your life who have had a positive influence on you. Ending the day with gratitude prepares you for a restful night's sleep and teaches you to live with humility. Science clearly shows that practicing gratitude can and does relieve stress, anxiety, and depression and is beneficial to the mind and body.

A: Affirmations: Yes, these are excellent for the evenings. As I wind down in the evening, I use a different set of affirmations, but you can use the same ones you use in the morning. The idea is to shape yourself into the person you want to be by using the words you use every day. The repeated process causes a subconscious reaction in your mind, helping you to become more conscious of your actions and ideas. It all comes down to your reticular activating system.

R: Reflect: This one has been a lot of fun. This one alone has helped me be more appreciative of my day and the events that transpired. Additionally, it aided me in mentally navigating my day and ensuring that I performed as desired. This is the time to reflect on your day to see how you interacted with others and how you talked to yourself throughout the day. Awareness creates better interaction with those around you. Do not skip this stage since it will teach you a lot about yourself and those you surround yourself with.

E: Embrace: I've always struggled with this one since I feel like I'm always "on." I'm constantly thinking about the future of Lab Coat Agents, A Brilliant Tribe, Tristan and Associates, Brilliant Thoughts, and my other businesses. At this time, I entirely succumb to the evening and stop! I accept that the day has come to an end and that I have done everything I can. Embracing the evening allows me to accept that I will be spending the evening with my family and friends. I still battle with this from time to time and check my email or notes from earlier in the day, but I catch myself and put things away. Embracing the evening completely will help you calm your mind in preparation for the next day's engagement.

That's it in a super concise process. You can choose to modify the stages as you like or follow them just like I have them. The idea behind the routine is to control what you focus on daily as you wrap up the day so that you are preparing to have an amazing day ahead.

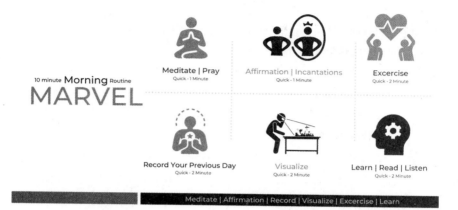

MARVEL

This one starts when you wake up, but I'm not telling you to wake up at 4 a.m. or even 5 a.m. I just want you to wake up with enough time to fit this in. If it's 30 minutes before your normal time, then that's what you need to do. Listen, change takes effort, so don't complain about what you need to do. Just follow the routine and let the process elevate you.

> **M: Meditation** (mediation/prayer or both): I begin with this one because it is critical to begin each day with a clear mind and focused thoughts. If you choose to meditate, I recommend beginning with the simple act

of sitting up straight and breathing in and out, focusing solely on your breathing. Additionally, I would recommend that you use an app such as Calm to guide you through the meditation process. The research on learning how to focus is immense and wide and will change your life drastically for the better.

A: Affirmation (mantra, incantations, or all three): The words you use to speak to yourself are significant, which is why this section is so important. I use affirmations to motivate myself to work on areas where I want to improve. Self, family, leadership, and so forth. I usually read through these in about two minutes.

R: Record: I've been journaling consistently since 2011, and it truly helps me clear my mind by organizing my thoughts and reflecting on the events of the previous day. I usually jot down what I did the previous day and keep my journal in an app called DayOne. Typically, I spend around three minutes on this. You can record your voice, a video, type it, write it, or just add pictures.

V: Visualize: I've shaped this section over the years into something I love. For years, I struggled with this one because everything I read and discovered online about visualizing felt wrong for me. I use this time to visualize the type of person, parent, leader, or anything else I aspire to be and mentally walk through the steps necessary to get there. I typically spend approximately five minutes on this part. During the visualization process, I go through three thoughts:

- Self: mind, body, spirit, emotions;
- Family: spouse, kids, siblings, parents; friends

- Business.

When I go through these processes, I allow my subconscious to inform me of which one I am most lacking in. I then immediately visualize two things:

- What can I do today to work on this?
- Where do I want to be three months from now with this?

Although this process can be completed in as little as five minutes, it can also take much longer.

E: Exercise: I've simplified this section for you. You can either use this time to exercise in the morning or do a small amount of exercise during this time. Because I exercise in the middle of the day to accommodate my schedule, this morning's session consists of two quick sets of pushups, totaling approximately 80 pushups. I occasionally perform jumping jacks as well, but only briefly to pump myself up and get my mind and body moving in unison. A few of my friends do burpees, but I'm not that crazy.

L: Learn: Usually, I use this time to read a book. If I find myself with only three to five minutes, I open my favorite book, *The Daily Stoic*, and read a brief excerpt. If I have 15–30 minutes to spare, I usually pick up the book I'm currently reading and dive in. Additionally, you can take a few minutes to listen to a podcast, a webinar, or watch a brief inspirational video on YouTube, Masterclass, or TED. I usually allot about 20 minutes for this section.

The morning routine isn't revolutionary, but the simplification of it along with the idea that you can do it whenever you wake up is something that I believe is important. Don't force yourself to wake up at 3 a.m. when you normally wake up at 7 a.m. I want you to wake up slightly earlier to fit this in because I know that small changes to your routine over a long period of time will change your life drastically.

Putting It All Together

When it comes to preparation, I believe that it should always begin the previous day. Being prepared for the day's events requires planning and reflection. In one of the *A Brilliant Tribe* newsletters, I outlined several questions you should ask yourself each day. In fact, I have two sets of them. I'd like to share with you the evening and morning questions you should be asking yourself.

Mentally preparing for the following day through reflection and active awareness is a skill that few people practice. During the COVID-19 period in 2020, I used that time to reflect deeper on critical questions we should be asking ourselves in order to prepare our minds for the following day. Numerous psychologists assert that change requires two components: a goal and an awareness of one's current state to assess the discrepancy between the two. We are all familiar with goals but not with how to become aware of them. Allow me to assist you with that today. Here are some key questions.

Here you go:

1. Are you pleased with the way you lived your life today? Yes or no? This is the first question I ask myself nightly so that I can reflect on my feelings on how I executed my day. The answer gets you thinking about actions you performed well and what you could have done better overall. Where I want this to lead you is how you interact

with people. Did you treat people well? If not, what could you have done to connect with people better? It's a great place to start with awareness.

2. What's one situation I handled well today, and what did I learn from it? To help direct my awareness in the right direction, I encourage my thoughts to gravitate toward a section of the day that I did well on. I also ask myself what I learned from it so that I can begin to digest it more easily. This is important because some of us tend to gravitate toward the negative parts of the days, and we replay those over and over again. This negative type of reflection gives many people anxiety, so start with a place of positivity. Reflect on the good to start.

3. Were any of my actions motivated by negative strong emotions such as anger, hatred, sadness, self-centeredness, or pride? This is one with which I still struggle on occasion. I don't always like the answer when I ask myself this question, but it helps me become more aware of my thoughts and actions throughout the day. In fact, when I tested this question out with friends and family, they also didn't like the response. It made them think about where they could have done a better job. My wife said it was *"like highlighting the bad part of her."* This one creeps up on me throughout the day as I consider my responses to people and why I take certain actions. This is a very powerful question, but be prepared to feel awkward at times because the answer will not always be to your liking.

4. Were any of my actions influenced by positive strong emotions such as happiness, kindness, gratitude, or self-lessness? This is one of my favorites. After the previous

21

Your Routine Matters

question exposed the dirt and made you aware of what you needed to work on, this question prompts you to reflect on your goodness.

5. Was I a good example to those around me today? This question is the essence of who we are. We are here on this earth to inspire each other and to help each other grow, either by example, helping others directly, or a combination of both. The more frequently you ask yourself this question, the more aware you will be of your daily actions. Through the course of the year, asking this question will help you become more aware of your actions and your impact on others.

6. Was I aware of the emotions of others today? Oh! We're about to delve deeper into this. The more sensitive you become to other people's emotions, the easier it will be to connect with them. This question will make you more compassionate, more loving, and more aware of the true feelings and emotions of others. This one is difficult for many people because the majority of people don't take the time to listen, much less be empathetic toward others during conversations. What an incredible question to ponder in light of our current environment!

7. Was my energy level high today, and what can I learn from that? Finally, it is critical to be aware of both your body and mind simultaneously. When was your most productive time of day? When were you most productive, and when did you feel the most exhausted? Were you eating healthfully and drinking enough water? Reflecting on this will assist you in connecting your mind and body to comprehend how to work at your best throughout the day! This wasn't one of my original questions, but my

friend who runs a multimillion-dollar marketing **agency** suggested this one.

Now, let's discuss the questions we'll be delving into each morning.

1. What is your directive today? I use this to help guide my day so that the message I focus on will direct my day and keep me on the right track. I can't shake always thinking about WALL-E when I think of the word "directive." It always makes me smile.

2. What am I looking forward to today? This keeps me focused on the good aspects of my life, things that I am excited about. Starting off with a focus on "the good" helps kick-start the reticular activating system in the right direction in the morning. This one reminds me of something that Hugh Jackman said in a podcast with Tim Ferris. He said that he tells himself what is going to happen today that is going to be amazing and he tries to make that one thing absolutely amazing. If you haven't listened to that two-hour podcast with Hugh and Tim, you should do that this month.

3. What good can I do today? Again, focusing on the positive here. You're purposefully directing your mind to search for the good that you can do today. At first, this may not be something that comes naturally, but the more you do it, the easier it becomes. I call this the "Grandma question" because my Grandma would always remind me to be a good example, ***"Hijo, don't forget to be a good example today. Everyone is watching you."*** That will always stick with me.

4. Who can I thank by text, a call, a video message, social media, a card, or a letter? This is one of the most rewarding and feel-good activities you can do. I've sent little note cards to my kids, love texts to my wife, videos to my team members, gifts to friends, and so much more. It's a quick way to keep you going in the right direction and have you start your day feeling grateful for other people in your life. In fact, recent research from the *Journal of Positive Psychology* shows that doing good for others makes you feel better about yourself.

5. What will I do today that will challenge my current mindset to grow? OK, here's where we change it up. Now we dig in a little deeper and begin to focus on things that can help you grow. Do you typically avoid reading, listening to thought-provoking podcasts, or learning in general? What are you avoiding that could help you grow? This is the time to write it out and see if you can tackle it in a day, no matter how small the action is that you take toward pushing yourself to grow! On days I only have a few minutes to learn, I throw in a part of a podcast, or 10 minutes of an audiobook while walking or driving. Even if I'm not able to take notes on what I'm listening to, it's still better than not doing it at all.

6. What might I struggle with today and how will I deal with it? Here is where we think deeper about any possible problems you might have during the day. A tough meeting, a difficult conversation, a problematic situation, or anything that may derail you. We don't just stop there; I want you to push to think about the solution *before* you encounter a possible problem. We often live life reacting

to what the day throws at us instead of planning ahead and deciding how to react to tough situations before they happen. I don't often like showing up to work out, but I do it nonetheless. I know ahead of time that I'll be putting everything in the way so that I don't work out, so I plan ahead, and I have my shoes and my clothes ready. I have my workout routine ready (most of the time it's a Tony Horton workout, so I don't think about it), and I just jump into it because it's scheduled in my calendar. I solve possible failures before they happen. Is it perfect? Not even close, but I will try to do what I want you to do because it will make you more aware of the possible failures.

7. What have I been putting off that I need to work on and put into my schedule? This one is here so you don't ever let go of a dream, a goal, or something that you longed for but just haven't made the time to start or finish! This question is the reason I finally finished this book. I kept on putting the book back on the schedule because it kept on creeping up every time I asked myself this question.

8. How do I want to feel today? This one is so simple yet completely overlooked every day. It's up to us how we decide to feel. Choose an amazing emotion and stick with it for the day! Choosing how you will feel for the day is like putting on clothes. It's up to you what you wear. What do you want to wear today? What do you want to eat today? What do you want to watch today? How do you want to feel today? I hope that puts it into perspective. It takes time to mold the mind, but it's your

job to re-create and rewire how your brain functions. This is my favorite question to ask my kids, and yes, they hate it, but I'm going to keep asking.

Simply remember that anxiety is natural and that we all experience it on a daily basis at varying degrees. I would strongly advise you to spend time each morning answering these questions. They've aided me in becoming more aware of my emotions, actions, and thoughts, and they've helped me in developing a stronger connection with other people as a result of my increased awareness of other people's emotions.

Tech
Calendly

Part II

Show Me the Money

Chapter 4

The Bowtie

If you pay attention closely to the tech companies that sell you leads, specifically the big ones, you will see that the main focus they have is lead acquisition. They focus on how many people visit their website and how many of those they can convert to then sell to real estate agents, teams, and brokerages. It's not a bad model; in fact, that's how most of these companies make a ton of their money, but they're missing the other side of this.

I've worked closely with billion-dollar lead acquisition companies, and the main concern is widening the net they have online so that they can turn around and sell these opportunities to the real estate world. This is why the opportunity we have as licensed real estate agents is to put a big part of our emphasis on the other side of the bowtie funnel.

You're probably very familiar with or at least have heard of the term "nurturing leads." That term is commonly used to explain what happens to leads that visit either you or your brand. Businesses do everything in their power to bring in the consumer so they can transact but put significantly less emphasis on the end part of the funnel that creates long-term relationships and, in fact, creates the career that most real estate agents want.

I learned this lesson after knocking on over 15,000 doors in the span of four years. I met a lot of people, and my main goal was to find those who wanted to transact sooner rather than later. I paid very little attention to those whom I met and connected with. In fact, I did nothing with those people. I did add them to a newsletter, but I didn't nurture them, and I didn't create relationships. Here's the kicker, though. When I finally did connect with people who wanted to transact, I failed to keep in touch with them after the closed transaction.

I didn't consistently communicate with them afterward, and I didn't make them a "raving fan" as Seth Godin says. I didn't add value to their lives after they bought a home with me. I didn't make them feel special. I didn't incentivize them to work with me or refer business to me again, not to the depths that I would have liked. This doesn't mean I didn't send them cards, or I didn't invite them to an event here or there, I just didn't have a system that they would fall into as soon as I closed the transaction.

What I'm telling you here is that both sides of the bowtie are important. I need you to build out systems to create business opportunities for yourself, and I need you to take care of the ones who transact with you. You need to take care of them for the rest of their lives, and you need to make them feel that you care. In fact, you actually do need to care. I can't teach you to care for the people you work with, but I can teach you how to create a system that helps keep you in front of them.

When you execute this well over time, you will find that the bowtie will be uneven. You will be rewarded with exponential referrals on the other side of the bowtie. It's almost biblical and reminds me of the scripture that says, "*Well done, good and faithful servant. Thou hast been faithful over a few things; I will make thee ruler over many things*" (Matthew 25:23). Yeah, this can get pretty amazing, so like Short Round says on the rope bridge in *Indiana Jones and the Temple of Doom*, "Hang on, lady, we're going for a ride!"

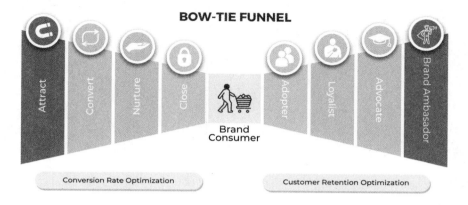

BOW-TIE FUNNEL

Attract — Convert — Nurture — Close — Brand Consumer — Adopter — Loyalist — Advocate — Brand Ambassador

Conversion Rate Optimization

Customer Retention Optimization

Chapter 5

The HOP Method

One thing I was terrible at for years was staying in contact with my past clients and my core sphere. I wish that in the first 10 years of my real estate career I would have kept in touch better with my past clients and my core sphere. Unfortunately, like many business owners, I focused on new customers instead of taking care of the ones I helped.

It wasn't until I got a coach who identified this as a big opportunity for business that I shifted more toward connecting with the people that already like and love me. I remember driving by some homes I had sold and seeing different For Sale signs pop up in the yards because I hadn't kept in touch. I had gotten so busy with new incoming leads that I didn't have time to connect with the old ones I had closed.

I don't want that to happen to you, so here's what I reverse engineered for you. During COVID I took the time to outline what has been working for my real estate business in California. First, I want you to understand how important this is.

Are you ready for some stats? Well, even if you're not, we've got to dive into this so you better understand our approach. Let's dive into your biggest source of income: your database, specifically the people that know you personally. They can be your sphere of influence, your past clients, or a combo of both.

Past Clients/Sphere of Influence

One stat that shows the importance of the real estate agent is the one by NAR (*2022 Home Buyer and Seller Generational Trend Report*), which shows how integral the real estate agent is to the home-buying and -selling process.

Eighty-seven percent of all buyers purchased their home through an agent, as did 92 percent of younger millennials and 88 percent of older millennials.

And when you dig deeper, you find that buyers are looking for specific guidance when it comes to real estate.

Buyers from all generations primarily wanted their agent's help to find the right home to purchase at 51 percent. Buyers were also looking for help to negotiate the terms of sale and with price negotiations. Younger millennials and the silent generation were more likely to want their agent to help with paperwork.

With a purchase this big, which happens to be the biggest purchase most people ever make in their lives, most people will look for someone they trust. This is why referrals are still the most important piece of the puzzle for success in real estate.

In fact, in the same report, we find that *referrals remain the primary method most buyers use to find their real estate agent. Referrals by friends, neighbors, or relatives were higher among younger millennial buyers (55 percent) and older millennial buyers (48 percent) compared to older generations. Older buyers were more likely to work with an agent they had previously used to buy or sell a home.*

If this doesn't convince you, then let the stat that says, *"Seventy-three percent of buyers interviewed only one real estate agent during their home search"* do it for you!

This means that most people who end up working with you as a real estate agent won't, in fact, look for anyone else to work with! Unless you screw it up.

It doesn't change when it comes to sellers either. In fact, it gets better.

Sixty-seven percent of recent home sellers used a referral or the same real estate agent they had worked with in the past. That number jumped to 81 percent for younger millennial sellers.

When you do a great job and you focus on helping people with their needs and you worry about the overall well-being of the client, you will be rewarded. Real stats don't lie. Take a look at referrals coming in from sellers.

The typical seller has recommended their agent once since selling their home. Thirty-eight percent of sellers recommended their agent three or more times after selling their home. That number jumped to 42 percent among Gen Xers. These are some amazing numbers, but here's the one that's the hardest to swallow for me. Here's where agents fail over and over again. In fact, here's where I failed for years.

Although *89 percent of* sellers said *that they would definitely (74 percent) or probably (15 percent) recommend their agent for future services,* a lot of them didn't. Why? Simple. Because we've never been taught what to do when it comes to follow up after the close of the transaction. We focus so much on getting the client and closing the transaction that everything after that usually falls apart because we have no plan, and those who figure it out either do it by accident or have found processes that work through coaches or training.

One of my friends does a great job when it comes to keeping these relationships strong. His name is Michael Maher, and he's the best-selling author of *The 7 Levels of Communication*. Check the book out when you can.

Those are stats for past clients. Can you imagine what would happen if we began to treat our sphere of influence (henceforth just "sphere," for simplicity), those who know us and like us, in a way that made them feel loved and cared for? Maya Angelou said it best, and many others have said something similar before her: ***"I've learned that people will forget what you said, people will forget what you did, but people will never forget how you made them feel."***

I can throw stats at you all day but let me tell you a story instead.

I was driving in the neighborhood of one of my past clients, and as a real estate agent, we love driving by and pointing at homes we've sold or even ones we've shown. My wife was in the car with me, and as I was preparing to point at the home I sold five years ago, I saw a For Sale sign. *Not* my For Sale sign either.

If you've been in real estate for a while, then you know this feeling. If you've been in that position before, you know the feeling. I was angry. The first thought was, *Why didn't they call me?*

The second thought was, *I'm way better than the agent they picked!* Yeah, that's called a "fixed mindset."

I was hurt. I was angry. As I let it settle in, I began to be angrier at myself. *What could I have done better? Did I not communicate enough with them? Did they not like me?*

I had a load of questions that all revolved around feeling sad and mad. That day, I decided that I would create a process for my real estate team so that wouldn't happen again. I would create a process that would allow me to connect with those people that I want to do business with, and I would stay in consistent contact with them, so they know I care.

As humans, it's easy to point fingers, but it's harder to take blame, even when you don't quite see it. In this case, I put my emotions aside and created a process that would level me up. I took full responsibility for losing that client. I also took full responsibility for taking action so that would happen a lot less in the future.

Here's the secret I want to share with you. When it comes to past clients and your sphere, most businesses can target them through three different verticals. There are more avenues when it comes to it, but here's what I outlined quickly for you so you can follow along. I called this **H.O.P.** It's an acronym that stands for ***"At home, online, and in person."***

Deciding who to place here starts with an understanding that all of your database needs to be categorized. *All past clients and spheres will be categorized as a letter followed by* "-sphere" (A-sphere, B-sphere, C-sphere, D-sphere).

■ ■ ■

1. A-sphere: Past clients and sphere of influence;

2. B-sphere: Clients/prospects buying/selling within 45 days or less;

3. C-sphere: Clients/prospects buying/selling within 90 (but more than 45) days or less;

4. D-sphere: Clients/prospects buying/selling within a year A-sphere (past clients and sphere) are your core: those people who have referred you to new clients or are close enough to you that if the opportunity presented itself, would do so. These are placed into the H.O.P. system so they are touched monthly.

● H - Meet them at home: These aren't the only ways, but these are some of the best methods we use to connect with our core people when it comes to meeting them at home.

- Through postcards, sent out monthly or quarterly
- Through handwritten cards (audience.co), sent out quarterly
- Through gifts from places like Client Giant (ClientGiant .com). This company does an amazing job of taking care of the gifting ideas for you and they all have different pricing options. Each gift goes out quarterly too.

- O - Meet them online (anything you can do with your phone): This is probably the method that has the most different approaches of all, but here are some that we use that you may like.

  - Remarketing: Usually on Facebook/Insta and Google, so you show up all over the Internet when people visit your website.
  - Newsletter: I would do a weekly one and use a company like Mailchimp or just use the email feature in Follow Up Boss.
  - Texts: Random texts of great quotes you read or pictures that show you are thinking of them. This allows for a deeper connection.
  - Emails: Not just property alerts, but emails with valuable articles to read that you find, or information about the housing industry. Different than what you include in the Newsletter.
  - Home search: Property alerts. Yes. All clients need to have property alerts.
  - Phone calls; To check up on them quarterly or every six months.
  - Social media messages. We cover this one in a later chapter.

- P - In person. This is the most popular one because it can be the most intimate and in some cases is harder to scale. I still feel like this one can be the most rewarding overall. Here are some options.

  - Annual client events (1–4 a year): These tend to be bigger like Santa event, Halloween event, 4th of July party, Easter Egg Hunt. . .

  - *Dinners: Invite 2–3 couples for a dinner each month.* These are smaller 5–10 people usually, and you pick a local lunch or dinner spot that is attractive and plan these monthly or quarterly for your best people.

  - Coffee/lunch: 1 person a week. Just meet up and listen to your clients. Listen and shut up and don't talk about real estate, just connect with people.

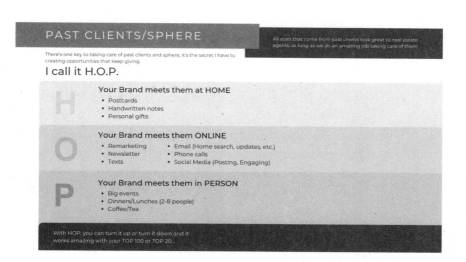

PAST CLIENTS/SPHERE

All stats that come from past clients look great to real estate agents, as long as we do an amazing job taking care of them

There's one key to taking care of past clients and sphere, it's the secret I have to creating opportunities that keep giving.

I call it H.O.P.

H Your Brand meets them at HOME
- Postcards
- Handwritten notes
- Personal gifts

O Your Brand meets them ONLINE
- Remarketing
- Newsletter
- Texts
- Email (Home search, updates, etc.)
- Phone calls
- Social Media (Posting, Engaging)

P Your Brand meets them in PERSON
- Big events
- Dinners/Lunches (2-8 people)
- Coffee/Tea

With HOP, you can turn it up or turn it down and it works amazing with your TOP 100 or TOP 20..

Here were some of the opportunities for each one of these three categories:

At home: Use handwritten letters. I recommend a company called audience.co that can assist with this

Online: Look into remarketing to any past clients on social media so that you can have a stronger presence online. Look at Ylopo or Chime for remarketing.

In person: I recommend taking past clients out to dinner in groups of about 20 at a time. Also have a photographer and video person there to record the evening. This will help you connect to your core past clients on a deeper level.

I hope this helps and it gives you some ideas as to what you should be doing for your business.

Tech
Audience.co
ClientGiant
Box Brownie
Follow Up Boss
Mailchimp
Chime
Ylopo

Chapter 6

Online Lead Generation

The Secret to Converting Online Leads

When I first started with working online leads, I gravitated to Craigslist. One of my friends handed me a PDF from the legendary real estate coach Craig Proctor. I read it and implemented it ASAP. Craigslist leads worked, so I did more ads and more ads until I couldn't handle the number of clients coming through.

I built a team around that, and then I pivoted to Google Ads. The year was 2007, and that's when I added an online layer to my real estate business. There were days when we would get over 1000 leads. Not only did I have to figure out how to manage that number of leads, but I had to put the right systems in place to convert at a high level.

I quickly figured out that I didn't want all the areas I was getting leads from, and I also had to put in place a quick way to connect with them. Not only did I find the best CRM at the time for filtering online leads (Follow Up Boss), but I also discovered a piece of tech that auto-texted incoming leads (FiveStreet, which I put in front of Realtor.com, and then they bought it and incorporated it into their portfolio).

ONLINE LEAD FOLLOW-UP:
THE FOLLOW-UP PROCESS
Single Agent or Team Member

Online Lead
(Google/FB)

FB/Google
Questionnaire
Answered

FB Lead Ads and Google PPC leads can have set questions and once answered by the buyer they will be added to Follow Up Boss

CRM

RE ADS
Automatically add every incoming lead to DARE ads (YLOPO is an option)

DARE stands for "Dynamic Ads For Real Estate. Recently changed to "Real estate ads." Created by Facebook, Instagram, and Messenger.

Automation (No Response)
1. Set to your own automation
2. Use Tristan's 7 Days of Love for FB or Google Leads.

Agent or ISA
1. Call within 3 minutes
2. Call again if no pickup after three rings within 1 minute
3. Text them right after voicemail is left.
4. Email them after text is sent.
5. Send nudge text 20 Min after last text.

After 7 Days
Turn on 1-Year Nurture if No Response from Initial Automation.

Home Search Set Up

Keep Nurturing
1. Be sure you check your tasks on your CRM daily.
2. If they engage often on your website you will see it on Follow Up Boss and be sure to reach out to them.
3. If you've categorized them as a hot buyer be sure to follow up with them every 3-5 days.

Made Contact
1. Change Stage to Contact, Hot, Nurture etc... Suggested use is A, B, C, or D.

*Depending on the automation you have set in place you will have **Action Plans** in your cm set to start automatically when you change the stage of the lead.*

A/B - Buyer (Ready)
Day 0   Text with self info
Day 5   Email I found this home
Day 10   Email the lending process
Day 20   Email under contract process
Day 30   Text article about RE
Day 40   Video about RE market
Day 50   Email location matters
Day 60   Text schools matter
Day 70   Email about home warranty
Day 80   Email example of home inspection
Day 90   Email example of contract

C - Buyer (3-6 Months)
Day 0   Text with self info
Day 5   Email home inspect. ex.
Day 10   Email video - RE market
Day 20   Email-meet me online
Day 50   Text open houses
Day 70   Email article about RE
Day 90   Email example of a contract
Day 110 Email video schools matter
Day 130 Text fixer or no fixer
Day 140 Email the lending process
Day 150 Email about home warranty
Day 170 Email video about local things
Day 180 Text don't want to spam you

D - Buyer (6-12 Months)
Day 0   Text with self info
Day 5   Email video location matters
Day 10   What's a prelim?
Day 20   Meet me online
Day 50   Text open houses
Day 70   Email the RE market
Day 90   Email article about RE
Day 110 Text schools matter
Day 130 Email home warranty
Day 140 Email video - the contract
Day 150 Text about investing in homes
Day 170 Email the lending process
Day 180 Email video about local things
         Text a home inspection report
         Text: don't want to spam.

Online Leads Flow Chart

As I handled most of the calls, I discovered the best approach for talking to incoming leads, and I took note of the different strategies. For the few years I was the main person making all the calls to incoming leads and doing all the follow-up. Yeah, I definitely didn't keep up. Today I still make calls to incoming leads, convert them, and send them to the team; I do it more for fun than anything else, because I have an amazing team that I've trained to do this well.

What you'll see in this chapter is a combination of things that work, and I want you to take what works for you and tweak it as you need. It's there so you have a starting point, and I want you to have a head start where I didn't. So use it, morph it, and then send me what you created because I want to see it.

Let's talk about online lead conversion, specifically leads from Google PPC, Google Ads, SEO, or Facebook. I want to focus on the process that we go through, from the inception of the online lead, up to nurturing or closing, or somewhere along those lines.

This is the flowchart of our process for online leads coming in from Google or Facebook.

I will go through the process step-by-step and answer some of the frequently asked questions I get.

Questionnaire

When a lead clicks on a Google or Facebook ad that redirects them to any of our landing pages, we have them answer a questionnaire. This helps us get a better picture of what the lead wants and where they are more or less in the real estate buying or selling journey.

Here is some of the information we ask for in that questionnaire:

- When do they plan to buy?
- How often do they want to receive property listings from us?
- Are they going to pay in cash or loan?
- Do they have a specific view they want for their home?
- Are they ready to view listings?
- Do they want to talk to a home search consultant?
- Do they plan to sell [their current home] before buying?
- How many bedrooms and bathrooms are they looking for in a home?
- What size, or square footage, are they searching for?

This is just some of the information, and I usually pay attention to the first two questions: The first one helps me see how ready this lead is to buy/sell, and the second tells me how often I should follow up so that they won't find it annoying or spam-y.

The more questions they answer, the better the quality of the leads.

CRM

The leads' answers to the questionnaires are linked to my CRM, and they are automatically retargeted for real estate ads.

We use Chime and Follow Up Boss, but there are a lot of CRMs available out there. I also got asked which one between the two that we use and recommend is better. The answer is: *it depends.* But if you don't have a website, Chime does offer both a website and CRM capability. If you already have your own website, you might find that redundant. You can use Follow Up Boss instead and link your website to their CRM.

Calling Online Leads

Ideally, you should call the lead within three minutes of them going through your CRM because their interest levels are highest while they are still on your website.

Imagine going to a store in the mall. If someone comes to you and assists you while your hand is up and you are actually looking, chances are you're going to buy. But once you step out of the store and you get a text or call later on, you are no longer as interested as when you were in there.

What most of us miss is that similar principles apply to online leads.

Another thing that most agents miss is, when the lead doesn't answer on the first or second call, sending them a text *and* an email saying, "Hey, I called you earlier. Sorry I missed you. . ." They skip this part thinking it doesn't work, but let me tell you, texts and emails do. Particularly emails. Based on experience, some of our million-dollar closings are from entrepreneurs, and they are leads that *check their emails frequently*.

So don't skip the text and emails, especially the nudge text 20–40 minutes after they click on your ad. Sometimes, people are in the middle of something when they see your ad. The nudge text increases your chances of catching them when they are available.

When you text your online leads, avoid asking yes or no questions. Instead, ask questions such as "You came in looking for a condo in Malibu. Are you looking for a beach view or one further up the mountain?" Give them choices that will prompt them to tell you what it is they are looking for in a home.

The main goal of your first call with a lead is to get as much information as possible about what type of home they want. This way, you can set up and streamline your home search, and you ensure that you are not spamming them with properties they wouldn't like.

The goal is to not be mistaken for a robot if you do send them a text or email. If they respond to you with "Stop," it means your messaging needs improvement. However, you can still save the conversation by lightheartedly letting them know that you are a human, not a robot, and that you understand the confusion because you've received tons of spam texts and emails too.

Lastly, once you do get them on a call, remember that your tone matters. Plus, the most important part is to pay attention to what they are saying. Don't approach the conversation to get to a close; use it as an opportunity to build relationships.

Automation

When it comes to automating follow-up and nurturing, some people think, "Isn't that overkill?" It isn't. Sometimes we get busy. By automating part of the process, we save ourselves time and effort. It allows us to show some clients' homes in person while making sure that we are touching our database. Let's utilize the tech available to us to simplify our lives and help us focus on higher-leverage tasks.

Final Thoughts

We won't get a close on our first call. Not even on the second, third, or fourth interaction. However, we are building relationships by giving value in each conversation. It sends the message that we pay attention to what they are saying, and we are catering to their needs at their own pace. They are the ones in control; we are just there to assist in their real estate journey.

You can't force a person to buy something if they don't want to. Your online leads might be a way away from being ready. They could be waiting for better interest rates. They might not even be sure yet where or what they are looking for in a home.

If your lead isn't ready to buy yet, that's okay. Focus on building meaningful relationships with them through the nurturing and follow-up process.

Your job is to give them what they want by using the expertise you have: finding properties that suit their needs and requirements.

Understanding Online Leads

We can either do paid or not paid. That's really the basics of it. Where do we go for nonpaid, and where do we go for paid online lead generation? There are some nuances to this, so pay attention.

The funnel: (1) Facebook/Google, (2) Google, (3) RDC, Zillow, Redfin, reviews, your website.

Google 5: Google SEO, Google PPC, Google Reviews, Google LSA, and YouTube, which we can dive into in the social media chapter.

I call this my **Google 5**. It's one of the core plans to put into place now to prepare your business for the near future. It's what I'm making sure the companies that I consult are working on ASAP. I've broken it down for you here so you can save it and put it into play as well.

UNDERSTANDING ONLINE LEADS

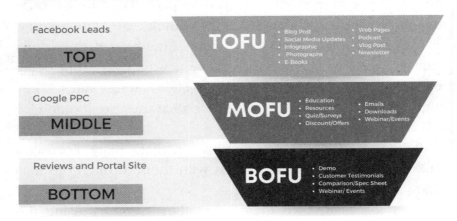

The Funnel/Google PPC

When you search for the most visited websites in the world you find that Google and YouTube are number 1 and 2, respectively.

Google has 92.5 billion monthly visitors, and YouTube has 34.6 billion monthly visitors, and that's a lot of visits. When you break down what other companies are doing to grow their business, they are investing a lot of time and money into the Google machine, and I want to break it down for you so you know where you should be starting as well. There are other amazing things you can do when it comes to Google, but here are the five core things you should be focused on.

1. *Google Reviews*. You've got to make it easy for people to find you on Google, and the easiest thing you can do for this is start a business page. It's called <u>Google My Business</u>. Here you can post offers, events, and respond to reviews. People can also find your business and call

Real Estate Prospecting

you directly or check out your websites. It's a starting point, and you need to work on this so it looks amazing when people google your business.

2. **_Google LSA._** <u>Local Service Ads</u> have been around for a while now, and I brought this up about two years ago. Google recently upped their game and opened up LSA to more businesses. By investing some money into Google you can show up at the top section of any search when people specifically search for your business type. Just make sure that you work on your reviews for Local Service Ads because it matters! The quality of the business you get from this section is amazing because the intent of people calling you is also high. Put this at the top of your list.

3. **_Google PPC._** <u>Pay Per Click</u> has been around for over 20 years. It came out around the year 2000, and it has dominated since then. Although you may hear talk about Facebook and Instagram ads, Google PPC still owns the market for ads. If you want to quickly break into any market, you start with PPC, and you will immediately see business come in. The key is finding a company that can help you create a strong campaign for Google Ad Words. If you don't currently have a plan, you need to put this on your road map.

4. **_Google SEO._** <u>Search Engine Optimization</u> comes in different forms, but the one that doesn't fail is when you create local content, whether it's in video format using YouTube or written content. If you are new to SEO, I would suggest you start writing about your community and tying it to a blog that has your brand connected to it. For example if you're in real estate, I highly recommend

that you create local content to specific areas where your business is and make sure you upload that content into a website that has a home search so people get local information and also make the connection that you are in real estate. *The key to this is to stay consistent over a very long period of time. If you write one piece a week, that's 52 pieces of content a year!* The key is to get started on this, and when you do it in a niche area you will see big results over the years.

5. *YouTube.* You've heard of YouTube, but for many businesses I talk to YouTube is still a mystery. What you must remember about YouTube is that any time a video pops up on Google it usually is a YouTube video. You must include YouTube into your business plan for the future. The consumption of video is the future of social media. Not only is YouTube the place most people go to when they want a tutorial, they now expanded to short form videos called Shorts! *Your plan for YouTube has to include consistent content along your niche for your business, and you must also put some money behind it.* You can do it on your own by watching some great videos on YouTube AdSense or you can always hire a company to do it for you. I've tried both, and the busier I've gotten, the more I have delegated this out. I still shoot the videos and I have my teams edit and promote them through YouTube.

Referral companies: There are so many referral companies out there now; I remember when it was only a handful, and now I can't keep count. The way referral companies primarily work is that these companies will send you an online lead, and you will work hard to convert them and win them over. Once

Referral Companies

you close the transaction you will pay the referral company that sent it to you a referral fee. That referral fee ranges from 30% to 35% usually.

The image above shows the ones I know of.

Newsletters: Newsletters still work; the ones that don't work are the ones that send out spam, things that people didn't sign up for. If people signed up to receive information about houses, they will open that one, and if people signed up to receive information about an area, they will open that one. Just make sure that your newsletter is to the right audience. I've got a few newsletters that go out weekly, and some that go out daily.

My suggestion is that you create your own. Make it specific to the area. Think of what Zig said about this: *"The great majority of people are 'wandering generalities' rather than 'meaningful specifics'"* and apply it to your newsletter; in fact, apply it to your social media too.

The portals: Buying leads can get expensive. I've spent a few million in my real estate career buying leads.

Google PPC/Facebook Lead Ad Online Lead Inception - The Funnel

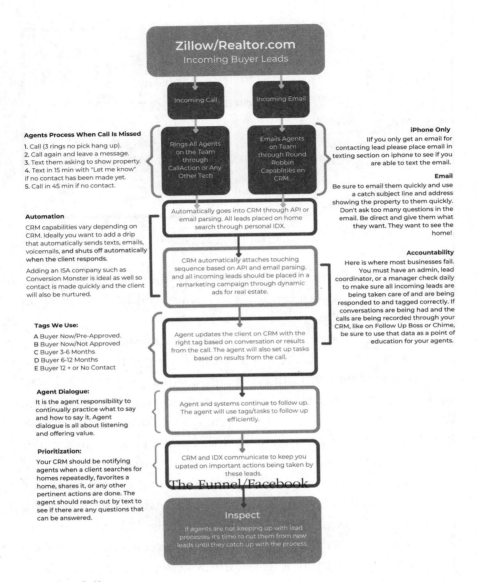

Zillow/Realtor.com
Incoming Buyer Leads

Incoming Call

Incoming Email

Agents Process When Call Is Missed

1. Call (3 rings no pick hang up).
2. Call again and leave a message.
3. Text them asking to show property.
4. Text in 15 min with "Let me know" if no contact has been made yet.
5. Call in 45 min if no contact.

Rings All Agents on the Team through CallAction or Any Other Tech

Emails Agents on Team through Round Robbin Capablities on CRM.

iPhone Only

IIf you only get an email for contacting lead please place email in texting section on iphone to see if you are able to text the email.

Email

Be sure to email them quickly and use a catch subject line and address showing the property to them quickly. Don't ask too many questions in the email. Be direct and give them what they want. They want to see the home!

Automation

CRM capabilities vary depending on CRM. Ideally you want to add a drip that automatically sends texts, emails, voicemails, and shuts off automatically when the client responds.

Adding an ISA company such as Conversion Monster is ideal as well so contact is made quickly and the client will also be nurtured.

Automatically goes into CRM through API or email parsing. All leads placed on home search through personal IDX.

CRM automatically attaches touching sequence based on API and email parsing, and all incoming leads should be placed in a remarketing campaign through dynamic ads for real estate.

Accountability

Here is where most businesses fail. You must have an admin, lead coordinator, or a manager check daily to make sure all incoming leads are being taken care of and are being responded to and tagged correctly. If conversations are being had and the calls are being recorded through your CRM, like on Follow Up Boss or Chime, be sure to use that data as a point of education for your agents.

Tags We Use:

A Buyer Now/Pre-Approved.
B Buyer Now/Not Approved
C Buyer 3-6 Months
D Buyer 6-12 Months
E Buyer 12 + or No Contact

Agent updates the client on CRM with the right tag based on conversation or results from the call. The agent will also set up tasks based on results from the call.

Agent Dialogue:

It is the agent responsibility to continually practice what to say and how to say it. Agent dialogue is all about listening and offering value.

Agent and systems continue to follow up. The agent will use tags/tasks to follow up efficiently.

Prioritization:

Your CRM should be notifying agents when a client searches for homes repeatedly, favorites a home, shares it, or any other pertinent actions are done. The agent should reach out by text to see if there are any questions that can be answered.

CRM and IDX communicate to keep you upated on important actions being taken by these leads.

The Funnel/Facebook

Inspect

If agents are not keeping up with lead processes it's time to cut them from new leads until they catch up with the process.

The follow-up:

I have two options: one that I run for seven days and one that I run for 20 days. It's an extensive plan, so we outlined it for you on our website at www.RealEstateProspecting.net. Go there to check out the 20 Day Touch plan and other lead campaigns for free.

Online Leads Scripts

Online leads require you to ask specific questions to discover what clients would like to do. The process below will hardly ever flow like you read it. You will most likely never get through all the questions, and some questions will be answered by the client before you ask them. Most of the time you will be skipping around, but the purpose of the acronym is to help you remember the right questions to ask in the right order: A MAID PLAN.

It stands for:

Area, **M**otivation, **A**gent, **I**dentify, **D**welling, **P**rice, **L**oan, **A**ppointment, **N**otes

A MAID PLAN—Full Script

Intro:

You: Hey (first name),

Client: Yes, this is (first name).

You: Hi (first name), it's Tristan with Happy Realty. You visited our site to search for homes and I noticed that you were looking at homes in X. Are you looking primarily in that area or are you also open to homes in Y?

Client: No, I'm just browsing. I'm not going to move. (Consumer)

Here you have two *options:*

Option 1 (credit to Barry Jenkins):

You: Looking is fun! My wife and I look online all the time, and we aren't moving anytime soon. What are you looking for when you move next?

Client:	We aren't moving for another two years.
You:	Got it. I'm always amazed when people plan this far ahead. I can't even plan dinner! (Hahaha) So, what is the plan exactly?
Client:	Well, we're looking for a house in _____ (city name), with three beds minimum.

Or option 2:

You:	Well, most people we help out are just browsing, so you're in luck (laugh a little). Look, I know you're probably never going to buy a home, and if you do, you're probably one or two years out. That's OK, a lot of the people visiting our site are. I just want to make sure I don't spam you. Is that OK? (This is a pattern interrupt. This approach is something different from what they are used to, and if done in the right tonality, they will talk to you, if they have time to talk.)
Client:	Of course.
You:	Awesome. I need to know what you like in a home so I don't send stuff that you don't want to see. I just hate spamming. So what are you looking for out here in _____ (city name)?
Client:	I'm looking for a house, a single story, three beds, two baths, (etc.).

Motivation:

| You: | Got it. I'll add those to your home search. What's bringing you down to this area? |

Or:

| You: | How did you end up choosing this area? |

Client: Well, my wife and I are retiring in six months, so we need to find a place that fits our stuff, probably a single story.

You: Great! Do you have an agent already showing you homes or sending you handpicked homes by email?

Client: Not yet; we just started our home search.

Or:

Client: Yes. We have one.

(Script created by Barry Jenkins.)

You: Got it. It speaks highly of you that you want to maintain that relationship and are bringing it up now. That being said. I've found home buyers that are looking on their own many times are receiving less than stellar service so they are searching on their own to supplement. Did you know if you haven't obligated yourself to any other agent legally, you can work with more than one agent at a time?

You don't want to ask, "What's the name of your agent that's showing you around?" because most pay-per-click inquiries or Facebook Lead Ad inquiries are at the very beginning stages. If it was a portal lead, then that question would be pertinent.

Identify:

You: I see. Do you need to sell a home before you make this purchase?

Client:	No, we already sold our home, we are renting for now until my wife retires, and then we are going to make the big move.

Dwelling:

You:	Perfect. Are you looking for a house or a townhome?
Client:	Definitely a house. We can't stand HOAs.

Price:

You:	Yeah, I get that a lot. What do you think your price range will be for the house?
Client:	We're thinking around $600,000. That is the estimate at least.

Loan:

You:	Very nice! Have you chosen the type of loan you'll be using or will you be paying cash?
Client:	Definitely a loan.
You:	Great! I'll have one of our local lenders give you a call in the next couple of hours to explain the different programs that you may qualify for. This way you get all of your preliminary questions out of the way.
Client:	Sure, have them call me after 5:30 p.m.

Appointment:

You:	Thanks! I've got some good information here to get started. I know you're a few months away from buying, but what's a good day and time for us to meet at my office (or a local coffee shop) so

I can go over the entire buying process with you? This way you understand the process well and you know what steps to take in the next year. I have Tuesday at 1 p.m. or Wednesday at 5:30 p.m. Which one is good?

Client: No, that's OK. I just want to browse for now. Thank you though.

Notes:

You: OK, well I'm like Google for real estate, so if you need me, just text me or call me. For now, let me go over what you're looking for one more time to make sure I have all of this. (Make sure you put in your CRM or in your notes.)

VIP Program: You can bring up a VIP program if you have one. A VIP program is one that would include any special lists you have of vendors like electricians, plumbers, handymen, etc., and also includes any discounts that you give your clients for working with you. Anything that you pay for that will help them when purchasing a home (such as a home warranty plan). Some agents also include a credit back to their buyers from the mortgage broker as well. VIP programs can be whatever you want. Before you decide to start a VIP program please speak with your broker.

Tech
FUB CRM
YLOPO
Conversion Monster

Chapter 7

Social Media

In this chapter, we go over all the ways that social media can supercharge an agent's business. Using a method I created called **STAY** and **LCM**, you can use social media to rapidly grow your business. We also go over tips and tricks for creating content videos.

The STAY Method

I frequently get asked, "What should I do with my social media? When should I post certain things and how often?" I created a social media calendar with the process outlined in response to the questions to make it simple for you to know what to post and when to post.

To make it simple for you to remember, I came up with an acronym. It is referred to as STAY. If you know me, I love acronyms and create ones for just about everything. It makes information easier to recall.

SELL WITH A STORY

It's time to show the world what you do. What you have for sale, whom you helped, how your company is doing, etc.

TEACH

This is where you help the consumer by explaining how to get a loan, what to look for in an inspection, how long it takes to close on a home, etc.

ADVICE

This one can be as easy as a quote about life or leadership or you can get into giving advice about something you are great at. Think of a hobby and explain how you do what you do. It can be gardening, running, gaming, etc.

YOU

At the end of the day, it comes back to you. Show people the things you do on a daily basis. Tell a story about where you eat, what you listen to, what you watch, what you think, and let people get to know you on social media.

Let's start with what each letter means.

S: Sell. It's time to show the world what you do, what you have for sale, whom you helped, how your company is doing, etc. For example, if you have an open house coming up or have a "just listed" property, you want to tell the world about it.

T: Teach. This is where you help the consumer by explaining how to get a loan, what to look for during an inspection, how long it takes to close on a home, etc. Teach other people or the consumer what you think they need to know. For example, how to get a loan or home maintenance tips.

A: Advice. This one can be as easy as a quote about life or leadership, or you can give advice on something you are good at. For example, what is your favorite hobby, and why do you enjoy it? It can be gardening, running, gaming, crafting, etc. I have an agent who loves gardening, so I advised her to show other people how she does it on her social media account.

Y: You. At the end of the day, it all comes back to you. Show people the things you do on a daily basis. For example, tell a story about your favorite restaurant. What accomplishment did your child achieve at school? Did you go on a dream vacation recently? Let people get to know you on social media. Show them your world. People will connect with you more if you allow them to.

The social media calendar that I have is something that you can use for your business. It goes through the STAY process to make it easier for you. It gives you great prompts to use, so you don't run out of ideas for content.

Don't forget to add videos. Try to incorporate videos as part of your social media strategy. For example, stand in front of a newly listed property and show your audience what you are selling. (That would be your "sell.") Then teach them about home inspections and what to look out for. (That would be your "teach.") Then give them advice—it can be as simple as a motivational quote or telling them about your hobby. (That is your "advice.") Then it goes into all about you—show them your furry friends or what you are eating for lunch that day. (That is your "you.")

Stick with the process. You want people to STAY on your social media. You want to attract people. The only way to do that is to follow the process. You can take this simple process to Facebook, Instagram, or even TikTok. You can do it all in a week or in a day, depending on what your target is. Do whatever you like.

Grow Your Social Media Using LCM
(Like, Comment, Message)

Let's talk about another acronym I like to use called LCM. If you're following me on social media, you may already know what LCM is. It stands for "like, comment, message".

Right now, you can do this on Facebook, Instagram, LinkedIn, and TikTok (depending on whether you are friends with that person and depending on the settings of the other users).

LCM is the tactic that I created that allows you to be able to connect with people at a higher level and also bring more people to your social media so that you can grow and that they can engage with you. I'm going to show you how to use it.

Here's how it works. We usually grab our phones to go on social media or on our computers, and we scroll through, leaving a "like" or comment on someone's posts. And that's where it usually ends. The problem is that when we think about social media, we tend to assume that people use it to post things in an effort to feel important. They want to believe that they are helping others and that people value what they have to offer. So, psychologically, you want to play to that. You want to stop having social media use you. You should use social media in order to connect with people and give them a sense of significance and specialness. And it's a simple process.

The thing is, you have to do this every day. As a result, I do this with my team, and we both do it for about 20 minutes every morning. We carry out this process on Facebook and all the other social media sites. It works for all businesses.

Now let me take you through this. I'm just going to give you an example from a recent post that I responded to on Instagram. I'll go through this process so you can see how it works.

This is a post from Dawn Cordiner, a friend and fellow realtor who I follow on Instagram. I'm going to start by liking her post. Then I am going to comment. Stay on topic and make sure your response is similar to what that person posted. I know Dawn is sharing her new logo with everyone and soliciting feedback based on her post, for instance. Therefore, I will say, "I really love the new logo."

My actions on her post now include liking and commenting. However, this is what will get me over the finish line. Here, I will be able to connect with people on a truly deep level and give them a sense of value and significance. This will make people stop and look at what you're posting, which is why I want you to do it.

They'll be interested in what you post on social media. What happens there is magical, because now you're hacking the system. That means the algorithm is going to take notice and say, for example, *"Dawn is checking out Tristan's profile and I guess it's important to show Tristan's feed to Dawn."* That's what begins to occur.

Next, I'm going to message Dawn. I'll be informal with my message because I personally know her. Something along the lines of, "Hey, I really do love your logo. It looks really awesome. How are your clients responding?" The key to making this work is to be authentic. My message is genuine, so it comes across as such.

This is where you want to make connections with people. You want to build relationships through social media. You don't want to seem like you're always *selling* something to them. You want them to check you out again on your social media platform. This is where the growth begins.

Dawn will read my comments and messages, check out my profile again, and perhaps "like" one of my posts. If what

I posted is good enough, then guess what's going to happen. She's probably going to share the post, too.

Now I know that I don't have to mention that I'm in the real estate business. Dawn will immediately recognize that I work in real estate based on the fact that she is viewing my profile.

As a result, we have to think a little bit more deeply than we usually do and explore social media more. You must include this in your business plan. You may think social media is a mystery and not know how it works. I'm here to tell you, though, that if you keep the steps in mind and practice them regularly, it's really not that difficult. You just have to remember LCM.

One last thought: instead of messaging, you can actually pick up the phone and do a video message. You can also text people. That also counts. If you follow them on social media and they are your friends, chances are good that you already have their cell phone numbers.

Five Must-Do Steps for Social Media Success

If you know how to use social media effectively, it can be a powerful tool for your business. Businesses can connect with their current customers, ideal clients, and potential customers using Facebook, Instagram, TikTok, YouTube, LinkedIn, and other social media platforms. However, you can only accomplish that by knowing how to engage with them, understanding how they can connect back with you, and building those relationships. Learning how to use social media platforms for business is crucial because it will increase your influence on customers' decisions. And here's a fact: even though the demographics of your clients or audiences may differ, certain social media platforms serve those needs. Facebook, Instagram, TikTok, YouTube, and Pinterest all have you covered, regardless of whether your audiences are late boomers, millennials, Gen Z, or Gen X. Social media is all about interacting with people.

I am going to lay out the five must-do steps you need to follow to succeed on social media. And yes, I'm talking about specific, actionable steps and tools. Here we go.

#1 Tell a Story

Selling a story is a part of the process. Look at the way Disney sells everything. There's a story behind the product. I want you to take a step back and think about how you can do a better job of selling with a story. It starts with telling a story about whatever it is that you're excited about or about to show. I get to do a lot of great content for Facebook, TikTok, and Instagram, and what I've noticed over the years is that the content that really connects with people is when you're saying something that engages people. So that's number one. Tell a great story.

#2 Tell a Story Using the 3 Fs

The story has to have the 3 Fs, which are: **Feelings, Facts, and Fun.**

Let's break it down. **Feelings** are emotions. It's about happiness. It's about sadness. It's taking your reader on a journey with all those feelings.

Facts are pretty easy. If you're in business, then you have data that you can share with people. Then they can share it with other people. Some of my best videos have been all factual. But we want to mix it up. We want to keep people engaged.

The last one is all about **fun**. The idea behind it is to keep people engaged for a long period of time so that they can stay with the feelings, they can share the facts, and they can have a great time with you because of the fun that you're providing. The fun is a little bit more challenging because it is so wide. Fun can be funny. It can be fun to watch you have a great time. It can be watching me have a great time. Or it can be just a great time all around for everyone. Being funny is a challenge for me. So I try to pick scenarios in which I'm enjoying myself or the people that I'm with are enjoying a certain scenario or situation, and that way we can film that.

#3 Who Is Your Audience?

I'm not sure people think about that fully, because now if we really want to dig into the audience, we can decide to do what, exactly, instead of saying, "Well, where do you gravitate to on social media to post about your business, to post about what you're doing, to go through that whole S-T-A-Y method." Now you're thinking, "What demographic is this?" You start to understand Facebook's demographics, which are a little older. And you think about YouTube. YouTube has a wide range. You've got older, in-between, and very young. Then you've got TikTok, which is for millennials and Gen Z. Then you have Instagram, which is more for millennials and Gen X. And then you've got Pinterest, which has a majority of females. Now you have to ask yourself: Where do I want to gravitate to? And is the message that I'm delivering, along with the story, hitting the right target? Now you have to understand as well how short are the videos. What is that graphic doing? Is it attracting the right people? Is it delivering the right message? So sometimes it takes a lot of work. This is why I have to outline a lot of things that I do, and I take the time to write them out. I ask myself who I am targeting. And I am going to deliver the right message. And sometimes I miss the mark, and that's OK. The point is, the more that you do it, the more that you'll figure it out.

This is why we did 100 videos in 30 days on TikTok. I'll use my social media strategy on TikTok as an example. Currently, I have almost 18k followers. That is posting three to four videos a day. Some of my videos have already gone viral. Both of the viral videos discussed a specific area in Malibu (where I currently do real estate) and had over 700k views. Another viral video had over 285k views where I talked about real estate trusts and things buyers should be doing, but they're not. What I learned from this is that when we're going in certain areas, people will engage with you and your content if they can relate to it in some way. Because of the one we were doing in Malibu, people were commenting, "Oh, I've been there" or "I need to go there," and they were sharing the videos. When you are teaching something, they usually want to know more. Like, how do I create trust? What am I missing? Tell me more about that.

We've been able to get business from all three different types of pillars, and that's where I want you to go deeper as you start figuring this out. You really start identifying with your audience and have a better understanding of the content that you need to create because you see people engaging. And that's the key. A lot of us are just scared of creating content. I'm going to tell you—just go ahead and put it out there. Let the algorithm decide what's going to do great and what's not.

My friend D'Rock says, "Your stuff is not going viral because it sucks." At the end of the day, if people don't engage with it based on TikTok, Instagram, Facebook, or anything just putting it out there, then there's a reason for it. Think about that approach.

#4 You Need the Right Tools

The right social media tools can help you market your business, connect with customers, drive more traffic, and even make it easier to sell products and services. No matter how big or small your business is, these tools can help you save time.

I'm just going to take you through some of the tools that I have used in the past or currently use.

Canva is the best place to start. I strongly recommend giving Canva a try if you haven't already. There are a lot of things you can do here with regard to your social media. Each social media platform's tools are available in Canva's library, along with gorgeous graphics and expertly crafted layouts. With Canva's simple-to-use format, you can really step up your social media campaign.

Final Cut Pro is another tool that you can use, and it's great for video editing. Final Cut Pro is a fantastic tool for video editors who prefer working on Macs. Powerful tools, such as filters, motion graphics, special effects, and more, are available in this professional video editing app.

Adobe Premiere Rush helps you create the best videos for all your platforms, including YouTube, Instagram, and Facebook. You can amplify your posts with easy-to-use audio and video editing software.

Viva Video is another one that I like to use. It's a popular video editing application for Android and iOS. It is an excellent application, and you can do almost any type of video editing by using it.

Hootsuite is technically a hybrid social media tool, as it can be used for scheduling, managing, analyzing, and social commerce. But it especially excels as a social media scheduling tool.

BuzzSumo is a powerful social media tool that offers data and analysis for you to use in creating your social media and content strategy. You can use the platform to see how well your posts and accounts are performing, including information on how many people have interacted with your posts and who and where they are shared.

As you can see, social media tools can assist you in streamlining your workflow, creating visual content, keeping track of your online activity, and ensuring that your content is seen by the right audience at the right time.

#5 The Ability to Delegate

Now, I can edit videos if I need to. I have the ability to do that. Is it fun for me? No, it's not. It actually takes me a very long time to edit and produce my own videos. I had to learn Final Cut Pro, and that wasn't very fun for me. I actually hate editing. So this is why I hired a team of editors. The idea of delegation is something that you need to take a look at, whether you hire one editor or a team of editors or content writers. Without my team, I couldn't be writing this book right now. It is something that has allowed me to grow so much. You should be taking it more seriously because delegation, especially for social media, can help you grow and can really help that perception of what you want everyone out there to see and that you're everywhere on all social media platforms and doing it consistently.

Creating Video Content

I typically split this process up when I'm shooting video for any social media platform.

First, I will take one day to write about what the video is going to be about. On the second day, I block time to actually shoot the video. This is key for me in creating content so that I have time to create and time to shoot.

I have five things that you should keep in mind when creating video content. Here we go.

#1 Choose Your Niche

Your niche should revolve around the 3 Fs, which we mentioned earlier in the chapter: facts, feelings, and fun. When you revolve it around the 3 Fs, you know you're hitting those points that people usually tune into. This is important because as you engage people, they stick around and look for more. For me, I usually go for the niche of teaching, whether it's to the consumer or to the real estate agent. I also like to use inspiration, leadership, and technology as a niche, or I will combine all of those. I don't dance, and I don't think that I'm funny, so it's hard for me to figure out where to fit that in. So I stick to the things that I'm great at. And so should you. Find your niche. Whatever that is.

Don't forget to go through the STAY process when creating your content.

#2 Outline Your Video

In order for you to succeed at a high level when you want to create content, you have to take the time to research it, do a one-liner, and then riff on it. You can repurpose the outline and use it on all your social media platforms. You can vary the time length as well.

#3 Choose a Different Day for Shooting

I don't like to shoot videos on the same day that I outline the video. Of course, you can shoot on the same day as you prepare your outline and scripts if that suits you better. I just like to shoot all my videos on the same day every week.

#4 Send Your Videos to the Editing Team

I made this mistake of editing everything myself for the first year. I am going to recommend that you don't do that. Focus on the things that you do well, like selling real estate. Leave it to your team to edit your videos. You can start out by hiring someone on Fiverr or Upwork to edit your videos. Once you expand your business and start making money, you can hire an in-house person to do your editing. If you're just getting started, outsourcing is a little less expensive. Now I employ a seven-person editing team for all my businesses.

Now there is a process for everything that we do. We can take a longer piece of content and edit it into a shorter format. Or slice it up into several different smaller pieces.

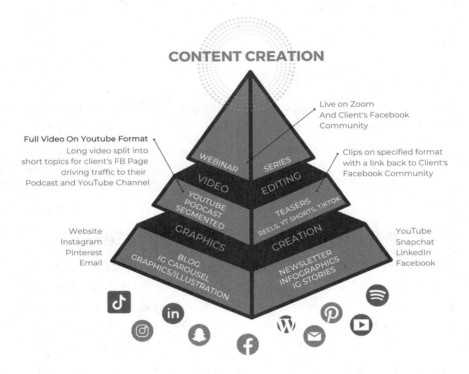

For example, let's say you have a video of a new property that you just listed. And you want to break that video down into smaller increments, whether it's for Facebook, Instagram, or TikTok. This is what we typically do: my editors come in and can pull the smaller bits out to use for newsletters, ads, YouTube Shorts, and TikTok. We can even make those into blogs. Depending on what you want to do, you can go really far with this. You have to have a plan. And more importantly, you have to have help.

Additional notes:

> Choose your outlet—Choose your strength and here are the main options you have: Facebook, YouTube, Instagram, TikTok, LinkedIn, Twitter, Snap, Pinterest, Clubhouse, and there are other ones, but I want you to focus on these, which have shown they have survived a few ups and downs.

Tech
Final Cut Pro
Canva
Adobe
Viva Video
Hootsuite
BuzzSumo

Chapter 8

Your Database

L et's start by talking, what is your database? A lot of us overthink and say, "I don't have a database." Well, guess what? You do. It's called your phone. And if everyone you know on there is still on your phone only and not in a customer relationship management (CRM) system, then it's time to get them out of here.

One of the things that we love to tell people to use is MCBackUp. It's an app that you use to export everyone from your phone to an Excel spreadsheet. And then you can dump the file straight into your CRM.

Do you have a CRM? If not, it's time to get one, whether it's Salesforce, Follow Up Boss, or Chime. The challenge is the same. You have to use it to its full potential. Your database is like a directory of everyone you know or have talked to or who has visited any of your websites.

Your CRM is more than just a list of contacts. The data gathered from your transactions will assist you in running a more efficient and lucrative business.

If you aren't using a CRM to its fullest potential, here are my five rules that will help you develop your business into a gold mine:

1. Create a strong database.
2. Add to your pipeline every day.
3. Maintain constant communication with your database.
4. Ensure all contact information is updated and correct.
5. Support and service to all the prospects.

Let's break it down even further.

Create a Strong Database

Whether you are new to real estate or have been doing it for a while, you must ensure that your database provides a solid basis for your business. When establishing your database, keep in mind that this is your retirement income. Many agents have sold their databases for thousands to millions of dollars once they retire. Alternatively, they may be utilized as a referral machine to keep money flowing during their retirement years.

How do you begin developing that gold mine? Continue reading.

Add to Your Pipeline Daily

On a daily basis, you should be adding prospects to your database. It would help if you started with your SOI (sphere of influence), whether you are a solo agent or part of a team.

Your cell phone is already a wealth of information. So, begin by going through your phone and adding all of your contacts, including family and close friends. They must be reminded that you are an agent capable of managing their business! (Don't forget to use MCBackUp Pro for an easy way to download those contacts.)

If you're working in a team, make sure you discuss how you'll handle your SOI. Is the split the same, or is there an extra incentive? In any case, be certain that the SOI connections are labeled as your own.

You show your thanks to the team leader by adding your own contacts and leads to the CRM. Your team will assist you in promoting your SOI to easily win more business! By integrating your SOI, you guarantee that your database will become a referral gold mine.

It can be as easy as talking to your neighbors, going to the park, talking to people at your kids' school, shopping, going to the car wash. You talk to people daily; just be sure to ask what they do for a living and come from a point of contribution; see how you can help them.

Five new contacts a day is ideal. That's 1,825 new contacts to your database in one year. From that you should be able to get at least 1% to transact, either through a referral or a direct purchase. One percent is about 18 transactions a year. Can you do with 18 more transactions in one year? I know I can.

Let's go even a step further and do the math. The average home price in the US is $428,700. If you sell 18 homes at that purchase price (representing one side of the transaction) at 2.5% commission, that's $10,717.50 × 18 = $192, 915. You may have a split with your brokerage, or you may be at 100%—either way, that could easily be six figures in commissions from just making five new contacts a day.

Action tip: Include your SOI in your database today!

Maintain Constant Communication with Your Database

What good is your database if you aren't staying in touch with your clients? Every time you call or visit with them, add a note to your system. Every time there is a birthday, anniversary, new home purchase, or client event, your CRM should generate an action. Send a "Happy Birthday" card, remind yourself to send flowers, or call the client with a market update, for instance.

Every single person on your database should be on a home search that's tied to your website, which connects to your database, and if you can afford to do it, be sure to also remarket to them on social media and Google. This way once they visit your website searching for homes you follow them online just like Amazon follows you when you look at the latest running socks. We use Ylopo for that, but you can use Chime as well. You can also use non real estate–specific websites like Adroll.

Have your VA (virtual assistant) or admin assistant go through your database and ensure that all the notes are current and accurate.

Ensure All Contact Information Is Updated and Correct

Make certain to include all the important information when inputting contacts into your database. The more detailed the data, the more effectively you can target your marketing efforts to those demographics. Your database is only as good as the information contained inside it.

When a prospect or customer completes a transaction or a marketing campaign, you want to be sure of a few things:

1. They have changed their contact information. (For example, a new home was purchased, an EXPIRED was changed into a listing, and so on.)

2. They belong to the appropriate database category and group. (For example, if an FSBO item has just been listed with you, you move to the Just Listed category.)

3. They are on the proper database plan.

Support and Service to All Prospects

You may miss out on opportunities if you do not use the database to consistently follow up on your leads. This could end up costing you money. The most important piece of information you can enter into the database is when and how you follow up with your prospects.

Every contact you wish to turn into a transaction should have a "follow-up date" set in your CRM.

Following up with leads is the most critical thing you can do to ensure your database is profitable and making money for you daily, even long after you retire!

Lead Follow Up

The biggest challenge when it comes to follow-up is finding what to say. Some people never end up picking up the phone to call or text their database because they feel like they are going to say the wrong thing.

Let's talk about what not to do first. That's probably more important than anything else: what not to do when following up.

Don't call up your database and say, "Hi, I'm just calling to touch base." What the hell does that even mean—"touch base"? I have no idea.

Or even worse, "Hi, I'm just following up to check in."

Really? That's what you're following up with? Can you get more creative than that?

That's the issue with our follow-up. It's almost thoughtless. It's not genuine, and you're not going to connect to people. People can feel why you're calling them.

It's the exact same thing when you're texting. "Hi, I'm just checking in with you."

No! Let's be a little more genuine with our follow-up.

Let's learn how to connect deeper with people. You may be asking, "Well, Tristan, how do I do this?"

It's easy. Most of our clients, most of our database, most of our friends, our sphere, our past clients are all on social media, including Facebook, Instagram, and LinkedIn. You may even find a few on TikTok. (Hey, it's not all about dancing.)

Here's how to do this. Say you have a client named Joe. You are friends with Joe on Facebook, and you've noticed that he's just started a new job. You now have a reason to follow up with Joe. You can go to his Facebook page and LCM (see Chapter 7). Remember to **like, comment, and message.**

You should also follow that up with a phone call to Joe. "Hey, just saw that you got a new job with that marketing company. I wanted to say congrats. Have you started yet? How are you liking it?"

This is what you do. You now have a reason to call or text. And it's relatable to the information you saw on Joe's social media account. All of a sudden, this becomes a lot more genuine.

There is no more "touching base." Okay?

Now you take the news.

Another great example is keeping current on the news—whether that be local or national—about our real estate market. Take, for instance, all the talk about the housing bubble that was circulating at the time this book went to press.

Calling up Joe and saying, "Hey Joe. I'm calling all my friends and past clients and letting them know how this current talk about the housing market and rising interest rates is going to affect real estate."

Again, now you have a valid and genuine reason to stay in touch with your clients.

The bottom line is that if you put a lot more thought into it, you'll get better results.

Maybe you have your team calling clients now. And you're thinking your team sucks because they aren't good at this.

Well, they aren't good at it because you're not training them. Your ISA team sucks because you aren't training them on how to handle follow-up calls with your sphere and past clients.

It is up to you to say, "Hey everybody, from now on, when you call clients, let's be a little more genuine, a little bit more authentic when we are reaching out to them."

And no longer touch people's "bases" or anything else. Get to know them a little better and give value when you talk to them.

At the end of the day, when you're calling people, what you should be thinking is: How am I going to make them feel? How are we going to feel after we finish our conversation?

Or are they going to feel informed? Happy? Bothered?

That's what you should be thinking. Before you pick up the phone, first you have to pump yourself up. Ask yourself how do you want to make people feel when they talk to you before you even make the call.

How do you want to make people feel after you text them?

The reason why it's hard to pick up the phone and call our database is because we don't know what to talk about. Well, now you have the solution.

You have to try different methods when doing your follow-up.

Most people will check their phones for texts. I don't really pick up the phone unless it's an emergency. When you text me, you will summarize the whole thing for me. This is today's reality.

People are guarding their time more. This is why I say when you go on social media, you should LCM. It makes people feel special.

The one thing I want you to remember is this: when you do anything that has to do with connecting with people, think about how you want to make them feel.

Tech
McBackUpPro
Follow Up Boss
Chime

Chapter 9

Farming

Farming, or as many other fields know it, "canvassing," is how I got started in real estate. I still love farming; I just wish I did it better sooner. Farming entails interacting with the community in some capacity, whether it be through door knocking, mailings, retargeting, or newsletters. There are many ways to go about doing this, and I want to explore them all with you.

There are some statistics about farming that you should be aware of, and those statistics come from the NAR (National Association of Realtors). To help you understand our strategy and the reasons behind our actions, I'd like to share a few of those stats with you.

Let's start with this one:

> Sixty-nine percent of all sellers moved within the same state. For younger millennials, 81 percent purchased in the same state compared to 63 percent of older baby boomer sellers, according to NAR's 2022 *Home Buyers and Sellers Generational Trends Report.*

Why is this important? Because it matters in the marketing that you're doing. It matters what you're sending out and how you are communicating with them ahead of time.

Here's another one that is important:

For all sellers, the most commonly cited reason for selling their home was the desire to move closer to friends and family (18 percent), followed by the home being too small (17 percent), and a change in family situation (12 percent). Older generations were more likely to move closer to family/friends, and younger generations were more likely to desire a larger home.

This statistic is important because of the psychological aspect of why people want to sell.

Think about your approach. Think about what you're mailing out. What does that look like when you're mailing out your postcards or newsletters? Really think of it when you're talking to people in person and you know that certain people are thinking of doing certain things, like moving closer to family or friends. This way, you will know how to communicate with the marketing you're doing.

Let's look at more stats that would be helpful.

The typical seller has recommended their agent once since selling their home. Thirty-eight percent of sellers recommended their agent three or more times after selling their home. That number jumped to 42 percent among Gen Xers. (NAR reports, p. 127).

If they choose to use you as their real estate agent, you must understand this. Showing up is everything at the end of the day.

Guess what happens if we show up and carry out our obligations? The customer ultimately uses us as their trusted advisor. They will also refer us to their family and friends.

Do you comprehend why this is significant? It demonstrates that if you do this on a regular basis and present the message in a way that will resonate with the consumer, guess what happens? A trusting relationship develops. Regardless of what medium you utilize—whether it's on social media or actual postcards that you mail to them.

Now I'm going to show you what we do at our real estate agency. Our farming strategy is laid out like this. We send out about 10,000 pieces per month and have a total of 24 mailers in a year. **"The Top Five Books to Read This Year"** is the item we send out that receives the most feedback. **"Quotes on Making a Better Life"** also get a great response. You can check out the outline and study it deeper.

We also include some back-end functionality in our mailers. We are testing out four different things. One of them is a QR code and scanning it will direct you to one of our landing pages. We have another one, and it directs you to our home bot process. Our prospects start receiving these notifications from us when they register this way, and we are notified when they do. The fact is, we constantly conduct A/B tests.

The other part of this is what I really wanted to share with you. What I noticed is that we lack creativity when it comes to farming and diving deeper into our community.

Door Knocking

For this, we use the Chime app, which is integrated into every CRM and allows us to keep track of our door knocking activities.

Aside from door knocking, you've got to get a little more creative.

Don't forget to add everyone to your CRM. You can then keep in touch with the people you meet and keep track of them in this way.

This is something I learned from my first experience of door knocking: **you need to give them something, whether a flyer or a postcard, anything that will make people trust you**. You are an unfamiliar person. They don't trust you yet because they don't know you. And trust is crucial to everything we do. How can you overcome that obstacle? What can you offer these people to earn their trust in you as a complete stranger? How can you introduce yourself and capture their interest long enough to get your point across?

You start building a whole separate farm on a newsletter once you've broken the ice and, through the initial conversation, persuade them to keep in touch via email. This involves informing them of what's happening, keeping them updated on what's happening, and what's going on in the neighborhood.

You now have a second opportunity to touch them. There is no reason you shouldn't have a Facebook group for a community in the world we currently live in with social media and everything else. It could be a smaller niche, like a track home area, or it could be a wider range.

If you are door knocking and you got their email and you can keep in touch with them for a follow-up because they know you, now you can add them to your Facebook group.

Mailing

Sending a mailer is the next option. We alternate between twenty-four mailers throughout the year. Messaging your contacts matters. Now it is just a matter of tweaking the contents of the message. Talk to the customers about their top concerns; at the moment; they are worried about a potential housing crash or bubble and about home prices. We should address those concerns with our mailers.

When I spoke with Darryl Davis (author of *How to Become a Power Agent in Real Estate*) during a REDX webinar, he said something that resonated with me. *"Mailbox is golden—that's where you should be."*

Darryl suggests that you focus on mailings because everyone is fighting for their spot on social media. How many agents do you know that are mailing you real estate–related information on a consistent basis? Probably none. Because there is *no* competition out there.

Even though we do the mailing ourselves with an inhouse designer, I would suggest you find a company such as Hyper Farmer or Corefact so that you don't mess it up at first. We also use different phone numbers for different farm areas so we can keep better track of our ROI; we use a company called CallAction for that.

Here is my mailing process that I use called "My Malibu Process."

Mailing to a Farm

Start small

My Malibu Process (and I suggest you start with 12 mailers, not 24)

Farming Outline

(24 mailers total in a 12 months span)

6 local market stats;

4 things to do for spring, summer, fall, and winter;

2 things about who you are and what you've done;

2 top places to eat locally;

2 top places for dessert;

2 things I enjoy about Malibu;

1 best Local Parks;

1 top 5 books to read this year;

1 story about Thanksgiving;

1 quotes about making a better life;

1 top 5 places to visit in California;

5 simple steps to increase your home's value.

December - Who we are/things to do in winter (December)

January - Best local parks/top places for dessert (September)

February - Local market stats/quotes about making a better life (January)

March - Things to do in spring/top 5 books you should read for the year (February)

April - Who we are/top 5 places to visit in California (March)

May - Local market stats/5 simple steps to increase your home's value (April)

June - Things to do in summer/local market stats (June)

July - Top places to eat locally/things I enjoy about this neighborhood (May)

August - Top places for dessert/local market stats (July)

September - Top places to eat/local market stats (August)

October - Things to do in fall/things I enjoy about the neighborhood (October)

November - Thanksgiving story/local market stats - (November)

Local Market Stats

- Sold - How many homes sold last month;
- Active – How many homes are for sale;
- Median price point - Last 6 months of sold homes averaged together;
- How many homes active if there are different tracts in your area.

Things to Do for Fall + Short Description for Each

- King Gillette Ranch: This park features 588 acres of landscaping and Gillette's estate. The Ranch includes the history of King Gillette and also a Chumash settlement.

- Malibu Surf Coach: If you are looking for surf lessons, then this is the place to check out! With over 30 years of surf experience aka stingray will have you hanging ten in no time!

- Los Angeles Horseback Riding: If you are interested in a horseback excursion, then check this place out! Enjoy traveling the Santa Monica mountains and experiencing the breathtaking views on horseback.

- Malibu Wine Safari: Wine, friends, and exotic animals. Need we say any more? This is a phenomenal experience that will leave you feeling satisfied on wine tasting and adventure. If you go, take a picture with Stanley the giraffe. He will be thrilled to see you!

Things to Do for Winter + Short Description for Each

- Fishing at the Malibu Pier - 23000 CA-1, Malibu, CA 90265.
  - The Malibu Pier is dotted with the brackets for fishing rods and reels, and there is always someone patiently waiting for a fish to bite. The pier is also a pleasant place for a stroll, especially just before the sunset. There are several restaurants on the pier, offering fish and seafood, wine, cocktails, and great views.
- Tuna Canyon Trail - 2807 Tuna Canyon Road, Topanga, CA.
  - This trail features nearly four miles of gorgeous outdoor scenery for hikers, bikers, or even dog walkers.
- Malibu Wine Safari - 32111 Mulholland Highway, Malibu CA 90265.
  - Explore the 1,000-acre Saddlerock Ranch and vineyard in Malibu. Your guide and driver team will lead the adventure on custom-built open-air Safari vehicles. You'll make stops along the way to take in the scenery, taste local wines, and get up close and personal with animals you never knew were Angelos too: zebras, water buffalo, alpacas, bison, and even Stanley the giraffe.

Things to Do for Spring + Short Description for Each

- Malibu Coastal Adventures
  - If you are thinking about going on an excursion, then you need to check out Malibu Coastal Adventures. They have options including lessons for surfing, paddleboarding, and kitesurfing. They also feature boat adventures

for activities such as dolphin and whale watching, coastal and island cruises, diving, and fishing excursions.

- The Getty Villa and the Cafe
  - If you are interested in art, history, and architecture, then the Getty Villa is a destination for you. This museum features many different time periods and cultures in the world of art. You will leave feeling full of history and knowledge.

- Malibu Pier
  - This pier is open to the public. Bring your fishing pole and enjoy adventurous fishing. Or take a stroll and enjoy the blue Malibu ocean.

- Good2Go Adventure Tours
  - In the mood for wine and snacks? Then stop by Good2Go adventure tours! You will be able to tour with a guide and enjoy local vineyard wines with friends or family.

Things to Do for Summer + Short Description for Each

- Radfish Malibu: Looking for some water adventures? Radfish Malibu is a mobile beach service that provides lessons and rentals at all Malibu beaches. Surfing, stand-up paddle, kite surfing, and kayak.

- Saddle Rock Gardens: If you like nature, wine safaris, hiking, and tasting rooms, then this is a summer hot spot for you!

- The Red Ladder Gallery: Take a drive to Cross Creek in Malibu and preview Eamon Harrington's art. He is a local artist in Malibu!

- Malibu Bluffs Park: Stop by this gorgeous park in Malibu! It features a lot of fun activities such as baseball/softball, picnic areas, a playground, a soccer field, walking tracks, and trails. Also, this park features amazing views!
- Adamson House
- Malibu Library

Who We Are

- Our names;
- Our brokerages;
- Our family dynamic;
- Where we live;
- Our short bios;
- Favorite food;
- Favorite books.

Top Places to Eat Locally—Include Short Description and Yelp Rating (Part 1)

- The Old Place - Agoura Hills;
- Paradise Cove Beach Cafe;
- Nobu;
- Malibu Farm;
- Neptune's Net.

Top Places to Eat Locally—Include Short Description and Yelp Rating (Part 2)

- Saddle Peak Lodge: This restaurant has a roadhouse and hunting lodge-type atmosphere. Their menu consists of fish, steak, chicken, and other American-type dishes. The atmosphere itself is worth the visit and experience! Yelp reviewers chat a lot about the great food and give it a 4/5 stars.

- Sunlife Organics: This juice bar has amazing and healthy treats! This shop has juices, acai bowls, shakes, coffee, teas, and more. You will feel the warmth of the sun life community! Yelp gives this shop a near-perfect 4.5/5 star review.

- Geoffrey's: Opening its doors in 1948, this restaurant had guests ranting and raving about its food and aesthetics. Geoffrey's is one of the original Malibu restaurant establishments that continues to thrive. If you are a seafood lover, then this is the spot for you. Yelp customers give it a near-perfect 4/5 stars.

- V's Restaurant: V's is an excellent restaurant specializing in new American dishes and specialty pizzas. Yelp reviewers give this establishment a 4.5/5 stars. The outdoor patio dining atmosphere is exceptional!

Top Places for Dessert Locally—Include Short Description and Yelp Rating (Part 1)

- Le Cafe De La Plage (4.5 Yelp)
  - If you are an ice cream lover, then this is the place for you! Their ice cream is made locally by hand. Yelp gives them a 4/5 star review, and it is a must-try.

- SweetBu Candy Co (5.00 Yelp)
  - Stop by this cute candy store that has put itself on the Malibu map! The 5-star rating on Yelp speaks for itself. This local family-owned shop will leave your sweet tooth satisfied.
- Sunlife Organics (4.5 Yelp)
  - This juice bar has amazing and healthy treats! This shop has juices, acai bowls, shakes, coffee, teas, and more. You will feel the warmth of the sun life community! Yelp gives this shop a near-perfect 4.5/5 star review.

Top Places for Dessert Locally—Include Short Description and Yelp Rating (Part 2)

- Carrara Pastries - Agoura.
- SweetBu Candy Co- Stop by this cute candy store that has put itself on the Malibu map! The 5 star rating on yelp speaks for itself. This local family-owned shop will leave your sweet tooth satisfied.
- Malibu Yogurt and Ice Cream.
- Le Cafe De La Plage - If you are an ice cream lover, then this is the place for you! Their ice cream is made locally by hand. Yelp gives them a 4/5 star review, and it is a must-try.

Things I Enjoy about the Neighborhood

- El Matador State Beach and its natural Cabanas;
- Leo Carrillo State Beach Caves;

- Trancas Country Market;

- Lechuza Beach and its Peacefulness;

- Malibu is a wonderful place to be. We thoroughly enjoy the beach living pace of life. One thing in particular we enjoy about the neighborhood is the ability to eat great foods, enjoy the beach, and connect with amazing people all in one place.

Best Local Parks

- Malibu Bluffs Park

  - Stop by this gorgeous park in Malibu! It features a lot of fun activities such as baseball/softball, picnic areas, a playground, a soccer field, walking tracks, and trails. Also, this park features amazing views!

- Las Flores Creek Park

  - If you are a trail and flower lover, then this park is for you. This park features over 1/3 of a mile of walking trails and over 45 varieties of native plant species.

- Legacy Park;

- Trancas Canyon Park

  - Are you a dog owner? If so, bring your dog(s) to this park! This park features a fun and well-maintained dog park. Your companion will be very happy to experience this dog park. This park also features a great playground for the kids. A definite must-see for you and the whole family.

- Conejo Creek (North Park)

Top 5 Books to Read This Year

- *Extreme Ownership* - Jocko Willink;
- *Man's Search For Meaning* - Viktor Frankl;
- *Start With Why* - Simon Sinek;
- *From Good to Great* - Jim Collins;
- *The King and Queen Of Malibu* - David K. Randall.

Story about Thanksgiving

- Fun facts about Thanksgiving;
- Thanksgiving Story:
- In 1621, the Plymouth colonists and Wampanoag Native Americans shared an autumn harvest feast that is acknowledged today as one of the first Thanksgiving celebrations in the colonies. For more than two centuries, days of Thanksgiving were celebrated by individual colonies and states. It wasn't until 1863, in the midst of the Civil War, that President Abraham Lincoln proclaimed a national Thanksgiving Day to be held each November.
- Grandma's Apple Pie Recipe.

Quotes—Making a Better Life

- "Life is like riding a bicycle. To keep your balance, you must keep moving." —Albert Einstein
- "All our dreams can come true if we have the courage to pursue them." —Walt Disney

- "Leadership is the ability to get extraordinary achievement from ordinary people." —Brian Tracy
- "Sometimes you will never know the value of a moment until it becomes a memory." —Dr. Suess

Top 5 Places to Visit in California

- Carmel By The Sea - Stay at La Playa;
- Half Moon Bay - Stay at the Ritz;
- Coronado Island - Stay at The Del;
- Yosemite National Park - Stay at Ahwahnee;
- Laguna Beach - Stay at the Ritz.

Five Simple Steps to Increase Your Home Value

- Paint the outside of the home;
- Redo the front yard (plants and grass);
- Redo the flooring (carpet/tile);
- Professional stager;
- Paint inside, neutral colors.

You want to promote with mailers and then get on the phone and follow up with them because it's the quickest way to generate appointments. Conversations that we have are the leading indicators where your business is heading.

The secret sauce to mastering the telephone and scheduling three or four appointments from those mailers?

Be Committed to Building a Relationship with Another Human Being

You have to ask questions and care about the prospect. The appointment will happen by itself if you care about them and ask the right questions.

"If you are good at building relationships with another human being, the appointment will happen by itself. They will ask you to come over. That's the secret sauce." —Darryl Davis

Online Community

Create an online community using blogs and social media. A Facebook group alone is insufficient. Create a blog, share stories with readers, and keep them informed of current events.

Give them content that will be valuable to your audience by informing them about current events, important information, potential destinations for their children, nearby parks, and tasty restaurants.

Because you are genuinely attempting to assist them, the more you delve into that, the more you can connect with people.

As you engage in this online community, remember that it's not just blogs and social media. YouTube can be another great option. Take a look at what TikTok has accomplished in the past year alone. When you target a specific audience and include location tags and keywords in your descriptions, the algorithm finds people nearby and recommends your content or video to them.

Handwritten Note

If you meet someone, send them a note. When you knock on doors, you occasionally get to meet nice, friendly people. Those are the moments when you create relationships.

Maintain those connections because the one thing that no one can take away from us in this business is that it's a relationship business. Everything changes if you approach it that way, especially when door knocking, farming, creating value, and thinking, "I'm going to create a relationship with every person that I talk to."

Now, the conversation doesn't end when you stop speaking with someone you've engaged with. Don't just put them into your CRM and leave them to be automated. Sit down and write a note. Or use services such as Handwrytten.

Personalize it. Make it your own! What other channels exist that will enable you to engage in genuine human connection? Because that's what's probably missing.

Don't always think large scale. Think, "How can I go super niche?" and then grow from there. That's where you learn.

In my first few years of door knocking, I discovered that I was meeting 13 people per hour (living in average-sized homes, not the enormous mansions in Malibu), but does this hold true the following day as well?

I also discovered from experience that the people I will find in multi-million-dollar homes have a different demographic and are home at different times than the people I will find in condos and townhomes.

Think of all the possibilities.

Community Events and Public Relations

Let me leave you with this. Consider what community events you could host as you engage in this farming process more frequently and begin to gradually integrate into the neighborhood. How frequently do you want to hold events?

Although our real estate team isn't big on events, if you are, consider the holiday events. How are you going to engage the neighborhood? (Read more about this in Chapter 10, "Client Events").

Finally, keep PR (public relations) in mind as you develop, just as we have in farming. That's not something I believe many people do. When you hire a company for PR, they will put you on local news, magazines, and/or news stations. That's something you can consider as you go along.

The bottom line is, I want you to focus on farming. The environment you live in is evolving. You have the chance to get to know people and establish lasting connections.

I was reminded by Hoss Pratt, CEO and founder of Hoss Pratt International and best-selling author, that there are three things you must do to dominate any geo (geographic) farm in this type of market. And they are:

- Pick a neighborhood that is not dominated by another agent;
- Mail something monthly;
- Identify 20 percent of neighbors that will be selling in the near future.

How do you identify the 20 percent?
The criteria is:

- Owned home minimum of seven years;
- Is *not* dominated by another agent;
- Find a neighborhood that turns every seven years;
- Turnover rate of at least 6 percent;
- Market to 500–2500 homes.

And you can get all this information from REDX. REDX can provide you with all the data you need to get started with farming a neighborhood.

Hoss also reminds us that if you are struggling, *"You can turn everything around today. You don't have to wait six months or a year. You simply need the right niche and the right data targeting that niche."*

In conclusion, you must ask yourself the following questions: What does that look like for you? Where would you like to begin? Around your neighborhood where you live, like I did? Or do you desire a different location that truly inspires you? Just be careful not to get too far because you must consistently show up.

BONUS

As a bonus I have a compilation of text messages you can incorporate into your farming methods when you follow up. You can use these for a variety of leads.

Texting for All Occasions

Generic buyer leads from a website (if possible, use the city they searched in for your texts):

1. Hi [first name], you just signed up on our site searching for homes in [city]. Are you only looking in [city] or are you open to other areas? [Agent's name]

2. Thanks for signing up on our site to search for homes. I'm setting up a home search for you now. Are you looking for a house or a condo?

Portal buyer lead (Zillow, Realtor, Homes):

Hi [first name], thanks for reaching out about a home for sale through Realtor.com. Do you have time for a quick call now? [Agent's name]

1. Hi [first name]! Thanks for reaching out to us on [property address]. Would you like to schedule a time to see the property and perhaps others like it? [Agent's name]

Buyer lead follow-up:

1. Hi [first name], thanks for your initial inquiry about homes. Are there any must-haves on your home wish list? Where would you like to focus? [Agent's name]

2. [First name], thank you again for visiting our site [site name]. I have a couple new listings in your market and want you to have the 1st look. Do you have time this week? [Agent's name]

3. Please let me know. . .

4. I know you're probably super busy, but I want to finish up your home search set-up. Can you please let me know if you're looking for a house or a condo?

5. There is a home for sale that is not on the market yet that matches what you are looking for. Would you like to see it before anyone else?

Buyer lead gone stale:

1. Hi [first name], I tried reaching out to you a few months ago. Are you still looking for a home to buy? [Agent's name]

2. Hey [first name], I feel terrible that we never connected about your home search. Are you still searching for a home? [Agent's name]

Seller leads from a website (any website):

Hi [first name], you just visited our website in regard to your home value. I'm working on the value now, and I need to know if you've done any upgrades to the home. [Agent's name]

1. Hi [first name], I just did a home evaluation for a home close to yours. Can you tell me a little bit more about your home? [Agent's name]

Seller lead follow-up:

1. Hi [first name], I sent you an evaluation report on your home a few weeks ago. Did you ever take a look at it? [Agent's name]

2. [First name], the market has gone up since we last spoke. Do you need me to send you an updated evaluation on your home at [address]? [Agent's name]

Buyer/seller lead in your database with no contact for months or years:

It's [agent's first name], I noticed you haven't been back to the site in a while. Did I drop the ball? Were you looking for something different? [Agent's name]

1. Hi [first name], I tried reaching out to you a few months ago. Are you still looking for a home to buy?

2. Hi [first name], I tried reaching out to you a few months ago. Are you still looking to sell your home or refinance?

Referral leads:

1. Hi [first name], I spoke with [client who referred] today, and she mentioned that you are looking to sell your home. When is a good time to talk on the phone to get more details?

2. Hey [first name], [client who referred] asked me to reach out to you in regards to your home search. How can I help you? [Agent's name]

zBuyer sellers:

1. Hi [first name], got your info online. Were you trying to get the value of [address]? Or are you planning to refinance? [Agent's name]

Buyers who bought a home:

"Take me off your list. I already bought a home."
Three responses:

1. The last time we talked, you mentioned you bought a home. I have a list of some great handymen that I can share with you if you need it. Have a great day.

2. I know you mentioned that you bought a home already, so here's a link to give you the stats on the current market—this one's for Thousand Oaks, so let me know if you want a different area (put link here).

3. I know you're not buying a home anymore, but I came across this article on keeping your home in tip-top shape (put link here).

Tech
Chime
REDX
Salesforce
Follow Up Boss
HyperFarmer
Corefact
CallAction.co

Chapter 10

Client Events

Having events for your clients—whether virtual or in person—is a crucial marketing strategy that needs to be in every agent's wheelhouse. They help you build a business quickly and easily. It's a fantastic way to build rapport and renew connections.

Research done by Frederick Reichheld of Bain & Company (the inventor of the net promoter score) shows increasing customer retention rates by 5% increases profits by 25% to 95%. I don't know about you, but I would rather work with more people who already like me, so here are great reasons to have a client event:

Stay Top of Mind

It keeps you top of mind. In this cutthroat industry, repeat and referral business are essential. When previous clients and SOI (sphere of influence) are invited to and participate in client events, staying at the top of mind is more likely. Client events are also a great reason for you to contact their SOI a couple of times a year in a way that is selfless and that comes from a genuine place. You will never have to ask for their business.

It Shows That You Care

Your clients and SOI will be aware of the extra effort you made to show them you care by doing things such as going above and beyond. Focus on building relationships and occasionally remind your SOI that referrals are appreciated. Client events are a great opportunity to do this.

It's a Great Return on Your Investment

According to studies, you can expect a 7:1 return by contacting your past clients and SOI 40 times per year (that's with 36 contacts and four client events). Accordingly, if your SOI database contains 300 people, you can anticipate 43 closings each year.

Whom Should I Invite?

This is an easy question with a simple answer. Everyone!

- Friends;
- Family;
- Past clients;
- SOI;
- Neighbors;
- Colleagues;
- Future clients;
- Partners/vendors including attorneys, title reps, and home inspectors. (Bonus: They can also supply door prizes and giveaways!)

How Do I Get Started?

If you have an assistant, they can help you get started with invitations and marketing and planning the event. In the past, I've had a title company or lender partner to assist us with organizing and planning the event.

There is a list at the end of this chapter that will help you get started. But here are some tips to go along with that checklist:

Start planning early

Put your four client events on your calendar at the beginning of the year. This allows you ample time to plan and reserve space and order supplies.

Reserve caterers or food truck (or order food and drinks)

You can ask your lender or title partners to help you with products or the cost of the event. Some successful agents I know sell sponsorships for their client events, and they get to put their name and contact information on swag and banners in exchange for providing goods and services for the client events such as food, drinks, and costs for party supplies or DJ.

Have a checklist

If you have never had a client event before, keep it small and manageable in the beginning. As you grow your business, you can have larger events. Keep a checklist handy. Add to it every event. See our checklist at the end of this chapter.

Budget accordingly

Again, partner with a lender, title company, attorney, pest control company, etc. It will help you keep the costs down considerably. Just make sure to ask your broker for any advice on how your state and office handle this part.

Post to social media

Don't forget to include photography in your budget. It's worth it to hire a professional photographer. Upload pictures to all social media platforms and tag your vendor partners.

What Type of Event?

You can do simple events such as a BBQ or rent a food truck and feed the neighborhood. Or you can do a large-scale event such as renting out an entire movie theater or throwing an extravagant holiday party at a clubhouse. (We have an extensive list of events at the end of this chapter.)

What I have found that works best for me is a small intimate dinner with a few of my clients. I like to invite around four to six VIP couples to a local steakhouse and treat them to a nice dinner. I do this about once a quarter. It is an intimate event that keeps me top of mind with my luxury clients. I garner several thousand dollars in commissions from referrals by doing this. Most importantly, it gives me a way to stay in touch with my A+ clients.

Virtual events are another option. You can choose to do something informative such as home buyer/seller seminars or even virtual open houses.

Whether you hold an intimate dinner with 10 of your A+ clients or plan a large-scale client event, planning and promoting takes time and effort.

You should adopt a hands-on, proactive approach and begin marketing it as soon as possible. You want as many customers as possible to attend, and you want everyone to know it's free. You want your clients and others to know that you look after them before, during, and after the sale and that they can trust you with their real estate transaction.

To ensure a fantastic turnout, we've put together a useful timeline of preparation before the event. You'll also get suggestions to help you plan your own fantastic client event.

First of all, decide what type of event you are going to hold. Here are some ideas to get you started:

Client Event Ideas

- Holiday events:
  - Pictures with Santa;
  - Thanksgiving pie giveaway;
  - Halloween trick or treat or pumpkin patch;
  - Easter egg hunt.
- Small client events (25 or less):
  - Baseball game (major or minor league);
  - Intimate dinner party.
- Larger client events (50 or more):
  - Skating parties;
  - Movie night/matinee;
  - BBQ/wine tasting;
  - Luau;
  - Back to school night;
  - Movies in the park.

- Fun ideas:
  - Shred documents day (provide an industrial-strength shredder) Around tax day is optimal;
  - Garage sale;
  - Recycle day;
  - Gelato or ice cream truck.

Once you have your event and theme, you can start on a timeline. Right up until the event day, there are numerous tasks to finish.

Client Event Timeline

Before the Event

- Six to eight weeks before event:
- Select a date and location;
- Identify which team member will run event;
- Friend every client on Facebook;
- Post on Facebook every three days (Buffer can help schedule these);
- Retarget your ads to the emails in your database;
- Video blog about the upcoming event;
- Email link to the blog to the entire database.

Client Event Marketing

- Four weeks:
  - Call your clients;
  - Email your clients;

- Snail mail your clients (postcard/brochure);
- Post the event on your personal page, personally invite clients;
- Text A+, A, and B clients to invite them.
- Three weeks:
  - Social media posts (every three days);
  - Email reminder.
- Two weeks:
  - Email reminder;
  - Call reminder;
  - Snail mail reminder.
- One week:
  - Start confirming attendance;
  - Text A+, A, and B clients to confirm.
- Three days:
  - Confirm attendance via phone;
  - Confirm attendance via text.

At the Event

- Take photos (also with every attendee);
- Take videos (for future event marketing);
- Hand out postcards for your next event.

After the Event

- Give personal handwritten notes to those who helped at the event; you don't have to be the one that writes

them: use Audience, Handwrytten, or Adressable, and
have a machine write the notes with a real pen.

- Share photos in the newsletter;
- Spread Facebook posts of photos out over a week;
  - Tag the attendees and mention how much fun you had
    with them;
    - Email entire database pictures and links to the blog page.
- Call attendees to thank them for attending and mention
  the next event.

Here are a few scripts that you can use for inviting and following up with past clients for client events and other situations.

Calling Past Clients/SOI

First Method: Client Event Invite

You:	Hi _____ (first name)
Client:	Yes?
You:	Hey (first name), it's Tristan. How are you?
Client:	Great! Still here at the home you sold us!
You:	Love it! Well, I've been looking at my database and noticed that it's been a while since we have talked. I'm not sure how I missed inviting you to our previous client appreciation event, but we're having another one. Will you be in town this spring? (Or summer, winter, or fall.)
Client:	Yeah, I'm in town and would love to come.
You:	Excellent! How many do you think can come with you? This way I can RSVP you.

Client:	Three total.
You:	Great. You're in. We're going to text you as we get closer, and we'll email you. What's your current email?
Client:	*****@gmail.com.

This approach will only work if you have events, but it's the easiest way to call up your database, past clients, SOI, or anyone. People love being invited to events, and they feel a little indebted to you on occasion for taking the time to invite them to an event.

Second Method: I Have a Vendor

You:	Hi (first name), it's Tristan. How are you?
Client:	Good. How have you been?
You:	Great! You know I'm always looking out for everyone, and I don't remember if I sent you our updated list of vendors. I've got a great handyman, electrician, plumber, pretty much anything you need. Did I send that?
Client:	No, but that would be great! We need a plumber!
You:	Well then, I'm glad I called. What's your email?
Client:	*****@gmail.com

Third Method: Just Checking In

You:	Hi _____ (first name). It's Tristan. How are you?
Client:	Hey Tristan. We're good. Thanks for calling. How are you?

You:	Great! I was in the neighborhood a couple of days ago, and I thought of you. How are things going with your home?
Client:	That's sweet! You should have stopped by and said hi! Home is good so far.
You:	Wonderful. Have you made any improvements to your home so far?
Client:	We just finished remodeling the downstairs bathroom, and the one upstairs is next. We're just giving it a break right now.
You:	Great, that will increase the value of your home. Are you guys fixing it so you can refinance? Or just so you can have a cool bathroom? (I don't ask directly if they want to sell, it's too direct at this point.)
Client:	We aren't sure. Maybe refinance and buy an investment home. We are just toying with the idea.
You:	OK. Well, let me see what I can find for you.

Fourth Method: Asking for Referrals

You:	Hi (first name), it's Tristan. How are you?
Client:	Good, Tristan. Thanks for calling. How are you?
You:	Great! I feel like it's been a long time since we talked. Is your home still standing? How's your family?
Client:	Haha! Home is still up. Thank goodness. What's up?

You:	All is great. I'm in the process of growing my business, and you're one of the first people I call because I really enjoyed working with you. Do you know of any friends or family that are looking to rent, buy, or sell real estate?
Client:	No, no one has mentioned anything, but I'll keep my ears open.
You:	Well, if you come across any friends or co-workers that want to sell a home, would you please let me know so that I can call them?
Client:	Of course. I'll keep an eye out at work too.
You:	I really appreciate that! And if I can ever help out with giving you a referral for a plumber, electrician, or anyone else, please let me know.
Client:	Thanks, Tristan.

There is so much more that you can do for events, and a great book to check out is one by my friend Michael Maher, *The Seven Levels of Communication*. I have a friend who is a mortgage broker, named Scott Edwards, and he does an amazing job inviting hundreds of people to his quarterly events; he models some of what I do above along with what Michael Maher teaches in his book.

Tech
Box Brownie
Client Giant
Cole Realty Resource
Addressable
Audience
Handwrytten

Chapter 11

Open Houses

All agents should be holding two to four open houses per month, especially if you're a new agent without a solid pipeline. In fact, if you are a newer agent, I would even suggest you have six to eight open houses a month until you start getting more clients who are ready to transact. Without a doubt, if you don't have clients, your business will not succeed. Additionally, it's a fantastic chance to establish rapport with potential customers, become known as the top agent in your industry, and expand your business.

Again, open houses may be done differently in other regions, so be sure to ask your brokerage about any processes or rules that are in place before you plan any open houses.

What Do You Do When You Don't Have Any Listings?

There are several options for you.

If you are a new agent, reach out to agents that have homes on the market, and ask to host open houses.

Look for stale listings to host open houses. Listings that have been on the market for over three months may benefit from "new blood" coming in and showcasing the home.

Look for vacant homes to host open houses in. This works great, especially if you're in a resort town. Beach or mountain homes make fantastic open houses during the tourist season. You never know who may be looking to buy a second home or investment property.

Look for agents from out of town that may need assistance in hosting open houses. There may be an agent from out of your area that has got a listing and they can't justify the drive to do a proper open house. Offer to do it for them. It's a win-win for both parties.

Once an open house is set, be sure to follow the open house guidelines to succeed at a high level. We have ten things that you should focus on when having an open house.

Let's get started:

Create a short-form video (60 seconds or less) and email/text the video as an invitation to your database. Send this at least 48 hours before your open house. List a few things that you love about the home in your video, including location, unique features of the home, and other details you might find interesting. Put this on all your social media.

Tell me a story about it. What did the sellers like about the home? Don't just stand in front of the home and talk about the open house. You have to tell a story. That's the key. That's what attracts people.

Create a Short Video and Post to Social

A great way to get people into your open house can really be augmented with paid and organic social media traffic.

When you create a video about the open house and post to TikTok, Facebook, Instagram, and YouTube and boost your post, it gives you the ability to target your audience based on geography, income, children, age, and more.

Regardless of where you put the video make sure to put a little bit of money behind it. If you have Ylopo, Chime, or any other digital marketing platform, you can put some money behind open house ads.

You can also use Walled Garden to promote a listing you have and go all out with a nice landing page too.

If you shoot a video, make sure it stays to about one minute or less so you can play on all social platforms well.

Pay to either boost your ad or use the ads manager to create a great ad. My suggestion is to spend $10–$20 per day for a few days leading up to the open house.

The best days to run it would be Thursday, Friday, and Saturday if your open house is on Sunday. Always run it about **three days before** to your open house.

It typically takes Instagram and Facebook about 20 hours to do the "turnaround" for your ads, so plan ahead.

If you know you are going to have an open house, I would begin shooting the open house on a Sunday. Make sure you take the time to edit it properly. Then have it ready to go by Tuesday. Upload it to social media and make sure you have a strong hook to capture people's attention. That way, it will be ready by Wednesday, so it goes out on time. The whole process takes about a week.

Usually, $10–$20 a day is sufficient, but test it out. It could be as little as $5 per day. In some areas, you need to go up a lot more to get better results.

Door Knock the Neighborhood

Door knocking in the neighborhood accomplishes a couple of things. One, it gives you the chance to meet the neighbors—and potential sellers and buyers—in person. Hand deliver a flyer or personal invitation for them to come to your open house *before* the actual event happens. Maybe an hour before the open house.

If it's the first time you are showcasing the home to the neighborhood, there will be curious people. Once one For Sale sign pops up, there will be more that follow. This is your chance to find those people when you give them the flyer. If they bring the flyer over, they will be entered to win a gift card ($100, $50—whatever the amount). This shows that they are committed because they brought the flyer with them. If no one is home, leave the flyer by the front door. (Don't put it in the mailbox—it's against the law.)

Be sure to do this one and two days before the open house. So if the open house is on Saturday, you will do this on Thursday and Friday for about an hour. You are going to have a flyer with you to invite the neighbors over to look at the home.

So not only do you give the neighbors an opportunity to see your open house earlier than the public, but you also start building rapport with them, you connect with them. They will start talking to you and giving you information about the rest of the neighborhood. It puts you in the loop about the neighborhood and builds connections.

That's how you invite people to your open house. You bring in more people this way. A personal invitation via door knocking is a surefire way to make sure you have a good turnout.

Do a Mailout

I mailed it out to the 200 neighbors around the house. Just like with your door knocking flyer, your mailout would be an invitation for them to see the home before the actual open house.

They get to see the home before anyone else, and it makes them feel special.

Another important piece of information you can include on the invitation is that you will have food and drinks. Having food feels more like a party and is a great way to draw people to your open house. Another way is to announce that if they bring the flyer with them to the open house, they can be entered to win a $100 gift card or a nice gift basket.

This is the perfect way to bring in those you weren't able to connect with when door knocking. It's a second chance to connect with these people who weren't home or didn't answer the door for whatever reason.

Hire Someone to Put Up Open House and For Sale Signs

I hate putting up signs. This is no different. At mega open houses, you usually have to put up 50-plus signs. It's not fun. You also have to map it out and make sure you have enough directional signs. Then you have to pick up the signs after the event is over. So do yourself a favor and hire someone to take care of the signs. Make sure you have it mapped out so they know where to go and where to put out the signs. I usually pay someone around $100 to take care of this for our team. Remember that your time is valuable and is best spent doing other activities. It's time to delegate this task to someone else.

Pick a Local Vendor/Business

Pick a local business that can bring in food and drinks. Our team uses a local coffee shop called Ragamuffin Coffee Roasters. We pay for the coffee and breakfast pastries, and in turn, they advertise our real estate team on their social media, and we do the same for them. It's a win-win. Our open house attendees get delicious coffee, and we get free advertising—and so does our local business.

Bring in a Lender, Title Company, or Home Inspector

This can also be extra hands to help you out. They can help you field people coming through and help with the sign-in sheet. If it's a lender, they can help qualify potential buyers. They can also bring in more goodies.

Depending on the home and the type of real estate market it is, we can bring as many as 100 people through an open house, so make sure you have help.

Use Some Type of Device for People to Sign In

Protecting sellers—they need to know who is in their home. This is a security measure. If you want to see the home, you have to sign in. You can use Open Home Pro or Ylopo—they have a great open house sign in. Chime does one as well. Find one and use it.

Don't be the person at the front doing this. Your time is better spent talking to prospects and greeting them after they are signed in.

You can use an iPad to capture people's information or have them scan a QR code that allows them to sign in on their phone, and when they enter their information it comes to your CRM.

Use BombBomb

Create a video in front of the house.

Script to use: "Hey, thanks for stopping by the open house. I wanted to remind you it's the one with the (insert unique feature or address). Thanks for stopping by. I'll be sending you more homes and will send you an email."

You can also put them on an automated campaign through Agent Legend.

Here's another script you can use: "Hey, you came to my property over on 123 Maple Drive. Remember, I have those other properties coming to the market. I will send those to you. Thanks again for stopping by. Did I miss anything regarding your search?"

Send that link through text and also get their email address.

If you create it on BombBomb, you can see if they viewed it or not or if they opened it.

Shoot one video at a minimum.

Once You're Done, Upload the Attendees to CRM

Place all leads on a CRM. Don't have one? Get Chime, Follow Up Boss, or CRMGrow. All leads should be put on a proper drip campaign. Do a property search with their criteria. It's your job to follow up and nurture them. Send texts and videos. Be consistent. It takes time, like everything else. When they are ready, you are there for them. Don't have commission breath.

We have a full follow-up sequence for open house clients. Be sure to visit our website at RealEstateProspecting.net to check out all of our downloads and scripts.

More Open House Scripts

Open Houses—All Approaches

Greeting People When They Walk Through

In order to convert the people who are visiting open houses into clients, it is important to start off the relationship correctly from the very first moments. Even though there are many people who routinely visit open houses, keep in mind it can be a tense experience for many to walk into a stranger's house.

Before covering the items that help you convert buyers into clients, here are some of the methods that are absolutely essential to avoid:

- Having them sign in: Trying to get people to "sign in" to your open house registration is not the best method for getting people's information. You don't have enough of a relationship at the beginning to justify them providing you with their valuable phone number and email address.

- Telling them all about the home: When you start off telling them everything about the home, a buyer feels like you are trying to "sell them" the home. No one wants to be sold to, so allow the buyers to experience the home.

As you walk with them through the house, ask them questions about what they are looking for and tell them information about the home and the area. As you are closing them let them know casually.

You: By the way, our team has a list of homes that are off market; these homes are not on the MLS. Would you like us to send a list of these homes?

Client: Yes, but we have a real estate agent.

You: Got it. It speaks highly of you that you want to maintain that relationship and are bringing it up now. That being said, I've found home buyers that are looking on their own many times are receiving less than stellar service so they are searching on their own to supplement. Did you know if you haven't obligated yourself to any other agent legally, you can work with more than one agent at a time? (Credit to Barry Jenkins.)

Client: No, not at all. Are we allowed to work with two agents?

You: Ah! Great question. You are, but let's talk about the best options for you. How long have you been looking for homes?

Client: We've been looking for a few months now, and we can't find anything we like.

You: Makes sense; we hear that a lot. Maybe I can help you out. Did you ever go through the whole buying process with your current agent? From A to Z, showing you where you can save money?

Client: No, we never did.

You: OK, let me do two things for you. I'll send you a list of homes off market, and I will meet you at my office this week. What day is good so we can sit down and go through this so you find your home quicker and save money?

Client: I think we can do Thursday after 5:30 p.m., after work.

You: Perfect. Let's do 5:30 p.m. It will take approximately one hour, and we will go through the whole process. I will also show you homes off market and on the market too so we can get you into a home in the next 30 days.

Client: GREAT!

Tech
BombBomb
Chime
Follow Up Boss
CRM Grow
Ylopo
Bitly (QR code and link shortener)
WalledGardenHQ.com

Chapter 12

Door Knocking

I spent the first day I had my real estate license knocking on doors for six hours. I dressed up, put on my tie, put on my dress shoes, and went door-to-door. Later on, I discovered that in order to break that cycle of distrust, you must first give. Because nobody knows who you are.

When I first started going out, people mistook me for a Jehovah's Witness. People would shout at me through the door, telling me to leave. I would tell them, "No, I'm not a Jehovah's Witness. I'm just a real estate agent." Now, there's nothing wrong with any religious groups door knocking, but you don't want to have any more challenges when door knocking besides the challenge of connecting with people when and if they open the door.

Remember that many times you must get through a video camera doorbell nowadays, so be sure to dress for success. People will instantly judge you based on how you dress and talk.

I would give them a flyer with the neighborhood statistics printed on it while introducing myself. I would let them know that I was door-to-door canvassing the neighborhood while they were looking at the flyer saying, "I'm just letting everyone know what's going on in the area." I then requested permission to update them via email.

While you are engaged in conversation, and you see that they're friendly, what starts happening now is that you start building a whole separate farm for your newsletter. With the newsletters, you're letting them know what's going on, what's happening in the neighborhood, and all of a sudden you have another way to touch them.

Here's a sample script you can use while canvassing:

Hi! I'm _____ with _____ Realty, and I'm in the area letting all the neighbors know what's going on with the local real estate market (hand them a flyer of the local market stats).

Here's what's happening locally. Have you been following what's happening with the real estate market?

Who do you know that may have thought about moving?

Any neighbors or friends?

Thank you for thinking about that. Can I keep you updated by email so you know what's happening in our neighborhood here?

So you're probably thinking, "Does door knocking still work today?" It seems that everyone is obsessed with digital marketing. For good reason, right? Literally everyone you know is on the Internet in some way or fashion. Online strategies, as we've discussed here in the book, have a higher ROI. However, there is no doubt that having a personal touch is also necessary. Nothing can replace a face-to-face meeting, and it also helps build trust and rapport while showing that you are taking that extra step to build their business and make them happy.

I believe that to be a success in today's market, you have to have a good mix of both personal and digital marketing skills. Going door-to-door seems like an ancient strategy. But does it still work?

Let's take a look at door knocking and what the benefits are.

Low Cost

Door-to-door canvassing is no doubt a low-cost effort, and it does help you generate leads. Plus, it gives the prospect a chance to put a face to the name. If you use it in tandem with Pop Bys, open houses, farming, and local community events, it can slowly help build rapport.

Stand Out from the Competition

Very few agents are using this marketing strategy. If you make it part of your marketing campaign, you will definitely stand out from the crowd. Just add a bit of some new-school tactics like an online newsletter, a local blog, a Facebook community, and other small things that we will jump into in upcoming sections. You can always jump into our website to find out more information there too: RealEstateProspecting.com

Boost Your Brand

Knocking on doors helps clarify your brand. It gives you the chance to deliver your message in person, and they get to see your face. Even if you don't get an answer, you can leave your marketing materials with them.

Increase Leads

You have a better chance of getting an answer to your script when you go door-to-door. You'll get your message across and have the chance to converse one-on-one with a potential client.

Handling Rejection

Are you convinced yet? Now that you know the benefits, let's get into how to handle any rejection.

One of the hardest parts of door knocking is getting the door slammed in your face. Or facing someone who is having a bad day. It is kind of similar when you are cold-calling. However, it is harder to say no when you're face-to-face with someone.

There are a few people who will make your trip worthwhile.

If you have practiced your script and your objection handlers before you go canvassing the neighborhood, you'll have a higher chance of getting a lead.

One of the agents that I coached recently won "Rookie of the Year" at her office because of door knocking. She was brand-new to the industry and didn't know what else to do to market herself. So, she did her research on neighborhoods she wanted to door knock and just went for it. She spent every day knocking on doors. She ended up making over six figures in her first year, and most of that was a result of door knocking.

Door Knocking Tips and Tricks

Do research before you start knocking on doors. First, figure out what area you want to canvas. Starting where you live might be a good idea since you most likely already know the market. You are best knocking on doors that are currently rising in value (as most are at the time of this book's being published). This way you can entice homeowners with how much their home is worth.

What are the qualities and amenities that the neighborhood offers? A market area that is close to good schools, hospitals, parks, and entertainment usually ensures higher home values and better turnover.

Do a comparable market analysis (CMA) on some of the homes that you will be targeting. Know what has recently sold, what is currently for sale, and if the home is pending. You will want to give people the most accurate information that is available. Have a flyer to hand them with this information.

When is the best time to knock? During the daytime on the weekends is always optimal. Or you may catch people at home in the early evenings, although I wouldn't go past seven o'clock. With more people working from home during the day, this may be the optimal time to go. You may have to test different days and hours to see what works best for your area.

Whatever time you decide to go, keep in mind the weather. When deciding what to wear, business casual is always a good bet. You want to wear comfortable clothes and shoes, especially if the temperatures are extreme.

Come from a place of contribution. Be a person first, a real estate agent second. Be kind and courteous. If you give them *value* up front, they are less likely to slam a door in your face and take the time to listen to you. Thank everyone for their time, whether they choose to listen to you or not.

Step away from the door after you knock. You don't want to get up in their face or seem threatening. Position yourself a few feet away from the doorstep and smile at them.

You can tell it's going to be a good conversation if they smile back.

When you do get to have a conversation with someone, make sure you get their email address (with permission to add them to your newsletter) so you can add them to your CRM. Set them up on a drip campaign and send out a newsletter.

Always leave something behind. If they didn't answer the door, leave your marketing materials by the front door (never in the mailbox). Your market report for the neighborhood plus a business card is a good start. If you have any business swag like a keychain or notepad, leave that too.

And lastly, always follow up. After they are set up in your CRM, send them a thank-you note for taking the time to speak with you (handwritten is ideal). If they gave you a referral, also send them something of value (a gift card is nice) to thank them for that.

Facebook Communities

In the world that we live in now there isn't a reason why you shouldn't have a Facebook community page for every neighborhood you work in. When you are talking to the homeowner, mention that you have a Facebook group for the community and get their permission to add them to it. Think of things you can add to the Facebook group to engage the community. You can post upcoming client events, market research and data, new listings and solds, and introduce new homeowners to the community, to name just a few examples.

Door knocking is a great marketing strategy that is still proving effective today. It doesn't take a major investment, and if just one day of door knocking turns into a sale or referral, it will be worth the effort.

Door Knocking Package

This is what you leave with every person you connect with while door knocking. It's a four- to five-page sheet—you can staple or clip it together along with your business card. It doesn't have to be anything fancy, but you can incorporate Canva and use some real estate–related images if you wish.

First page: "How can I help you today? I value building relationships over transactions." Photo of you and/or your team with a section at the bottom with recent reviews (from Zillow, Google, Yelp, client feedback survey).

Second page: Your bio or resume. Keep this short and sweet. It's just an introduction so they can get to know you. No need to put your whole life story. Include more photos of you and your family or pets. The key is to make it personable.

Third page: Recent market activity in their neighborhood. Very basic and simple. You can use your MLS to pull stats. Incorporate what has sold in and around their neighborhood.

Fourth page: More MLS sheets, if necessary. If there are fewer than five properties, you can do a full printout of the MLS sheet. If more than that, I would do a "one line" sheet that shows recent sales, pendings, and activities.

Fifth page: "What is your house worth? Find out today. Call me at XXX-XXX-XXXX."

And that's it. Keep it simple but packed with valuable information for the homeowner.

Door Knock Script

"Hi, how's it going today? I'm Tristan with XYZ Realty. Don't worry, I'm not here to try and get you to sell your house, I promise. I don't want to take up too much of your time today. The reason for my knock is that I've provided you with a market snapshot. (Don't hand it to them yet.) And seeing if there's anything I can do for you right now or in the future? (Then hand them the door knock package.)

Now here is where you *shut up* and *listen*. This is the critical piece of the script. You have to listen very carefully to what they say.

Majority of the time, they will say, "No, thank you."

"No worries. Let me ask you this. Then I'll be on my way. If you were to move, what agent would you use?" (Don't ask "*Do you have an agent*"—it's easier for them to just say yes. Always ask *who*, so they have to stop and think.)

Majority of the time, they will say, "We don't have anyone in mind."

You: Well, I would love to be able to help you in the future if you need anything.

Client: Okay, thank you.

You: Would it be okay if I stayed in touch with you?

Client: Sure, that would be great.

(Use your pad and ask them their name and email address.)

Then thank them for their time and say goodbye. Unless they keep the conversation going, end it here and be on your way. You want to be respectful and not take up too much of their time.

Door Knocking Scripts

Just Listed or Just Sold Scripts

Use these scripts when you or your brokerage has sold or just listed a home in their neighborhood.

"Hello, I'm _____ with _____Realty. I just listed (or sold) your neighbor's home. Who do you know that would be interested in selling?"

"Hello, I'm _____ with _____ Realty. One of my homes in the neighborhood just sold. Would you be interested in finding out how much your home is worth?"

Higher Home Values

Use this script when home values are higher than normal, and you are in a seller's market or a market shift is coming.

"Hello, I'm_____ with _____Realty. (Hand them your marketing flyer with statistics on it.) Here's some valuable research that I've done on your neighborhood, and I'm noticing that the homes are selling at record prices (or way above the normal buying price). Would you like to know how much yours is worth?"

More Scripts

These scripts come from my personal vault. Take the time to role-play and put your own spin on them.

Door knocking—All Approaches

First Option

You: Hi there, I'm Tristan with X Realty. How are you? A home down the street from yours on Main St. just sold for $10,000 over the asking price and there were four total offers.So I'm out here knocking because there are some qualified buyers looking for a home in this area, and they can't find one now. Do you know of any neighbors that have talked to you about selling?

Client: No, sorry.

You: Thank you. We also have a few neighbors that have asked us to give them a quick value of their home. Did you want me to put you on that list?

Client: Yes, it wouldn't hurt.

You:	Great! Thank you for your time. I'll see if I can find these buyers a home locally. Have you given any thought to selling and cashing out?
Client:	No, sorry. I'm staying here for a long time.

Second Option

You:	Hi there, I'm Tristan with X Realty, how are you? I'm going through the neighborhood today handing out a neighborhood update. It shows all the homes on the market and the ones that have sold. (Hand them the flyer.)
Client:	Thanks, but I'm not selling.
You:	Got it. I was hoping that you could tell me if any of your neighbors have talked about selling?
Client:	No one I can think of. I don't talk to the neighbors much.
You:	I see. It's a great neighborhood. I don't live too far from here. Do you know anyone thinking of moving into the neighborhood?
Client:	Not really, it's too expensive for everyone that we know.
You:	Well, thanks for taking the time to think about it. I appreciate it. Before you go, can I add you to my monthly email that sends out local information about things to do, events, top places to eat, and neighborhood reports about local market trends?
Client:	Sure, my email is Me@Me.com.

You:	Thanks! I'll set you up this week. Sounds like you've been here a while. How did you end up picking this place?
Client:	I was relocating for my job, been here 15 years now.
You:	WOW! If you ever did move, where do you think you would move to?
Client:	Ha! Probably where I moved from. I miss Oregon.
You:	Nice, never been up there. When do you think you'd move back up?
Client:	I would probably do it in five years, but I would have to sell this first. It's a while from now. Listen, I have to go now, but thanks for stopping by.
You:	Yeah! Thanks for opening the door. Look out for my email. Talk to you later.

Tech

Knockwise: http://knockwise.com/why-us

Chime CRM app for door knocking

Get more scripts at www.RealEstateProspecting.net

Chapter 13

Cold-Calling

I know what you're probably thinking, cold-calling sucks or it doesn't work. Yes, I hear you, but bear with me on this one. If you ask agents what makes them successful at prospecting, they will tell you it actually starts the night before. A strong pre-prospecting routine is a key habit to hitting your prospecting goals. You will find it easier to build and maintain positive momentum during your call sessions if you have a regular routine in place before you pick up the phone. There are some things that a real estate professional cannot always plan for. Good habits that promote optimism from the moment you wake up are something you can control. Continue reading to learn the elements of a productive pre-prospecting routine.

Before you start calling just make sure you talk to your brokerage too, because each brokerage has a different take on how to approach cold-calling. Some have specific processes you need to follow, and some don't allow it, so be mindful of that.

Start the Night Before

Spend a short while getting ready for tomorrow's prospecting before going to bed. Lay out your clothes, create your call lists, and review your schedule for tomorrow so that you can get up and go without any unnecessary distractions. Go back and read the chapter in this book about morning and nighttime routines if you haven't already. I always review my tasks and schedule for the next day the night before—try it! You'll be able to manage your day better.

Get a good night's sleep; that is the most important thing! Avoid using screens, such as those on TVs, computers, and smartphones, at least two hours before bedtime to get about seven to eight hours of sleep every night. With better sleep, prospecting productivity will increase, and stress levels will significantly decrease.

Review Your Numbers

Every successful prospecting agent is fully aware of the number of calls, contacts, and appointments needed each day to accomplish their goals. If you're new to prospecting or unsure of where to start, commit to calling for at least 90 days (three to four hours per day, three days per week). You'll be able to create a reasonable baseline as a result. As a consequence, you will gain a better understanding of the realities of real estate prospecting, which will help you set realistic daily call goals.

Before ending his prospecting for the day, our ISA (inside sales agent) lead aims to make at least 25 contacts and schedule one listing appointment, Does this happen daily? No, but that's what we shoot for. To achieve his daily goals when our ISA first started prospecting, he had to call for at least four hours. After two years of consistent prospecting, he can now reach (or exceed) his daily goals in just a few hours.

I come from a telemarketing background, and before I would make calls, I would have a sheet ready to go. Something that I would track numbers with and save so I could see how many calls I needed to make on average to make one contact.

One other important piece to this is to make sure you know who you are calling. Are you calling a neighborhood to let them know you or your office has a new listing? Are you calling for sale by owners? Who are you calling? Make sure you have your dialogue set in place before you start calling.

Review Your Business Plan and Your Goals

Every day before prospecting, go over your daily, weekly, monthly, and yearly goals. Verify that they remain consistent with your business plan and are realistic goals. Adjust as necessary, and most importantly, never forget your "why."

Role-play

You have to practice what you say. I have frequently sat and listened to an agent when they speak to an expired or FSBO prospect, and they are at a loss for words. They lack the skills necessary to deal with objections.

Think of an attorney when they are making an argument and they get an objection from the opposing counsel. Does that attorney shut down or do they keep going? On the other hand, most agents don't know how to proceed when something unexpected happens. What you need to do is role-play, as was suggested above. When I first started out as a real estate agent, I used to sit in the car with my wife and ask her to role-play with me. I wasn't that great at it—at least she didn't tell me that I sucked—but I would practice what to say as if I were speaking to a homeowner.

After you review your goals and prepare your numbers, make sure you set aside 30 minutes every morning to role-play with your accountability partner (if you have one).

The best way to internalize your scripts, practice challenging objections, and receive helpful feedback from other agents is to practice role-playing every day. You can do this with your team or brokerage, as well as in online real estate groups where you can find good role-play partners.

Make sure to role-play every day as part of your pre-prospecting routine, regardless of who you practice with. Before making calls to your leads, it will help you get comfortable and get those first few uncomfortable conversations out of the way.

One great thing that helped me was recording my dialogue and then replaying it back so I could catch my little quirks and get better at what I would say to customers. Try it; you can do it with your cell phone easily and create folders on your recordings so you can go back and listen as you get better.

Use a Mindset Strategy for a Confidence Boost

Affirmations

This may sound super crazy or silly for some of you, but let me explain the reasoning here. We all have a negative little voice in our heads that says things like, "That was stupid, why can't you do better? I just can't do this anymore. . ." What I've noticed over the years is that we can replace those words if we are purposeful with how we talk to ourselves daily.

This is where affirmations come into play. You choose how you talk to yourself, you choose the words you use instead of letting the situation dictate how you feel. This allows you to keep going without sabotaging or second-guessing yourself.

Using positive affirmations can help clear your mind and give yourself an extra boost of confidence. Reciting affirmations before prospecting is a great way to establish your mindset and reduce call-making anxiety.

Make sure your affirmations are in line with your habits and goals for prospecting. Daily affirmations will strengthen your prospecting attitude as they become automatic after enough practice and time. Affirmations should be written and said in the present tense, as if you've already achieved your goal. Here are a few we recommend you can use to get started (revise in order to fit your needs):

- I am ready to help my prospects!
- I manage my time effectively.
- I practice my sales scripts daily.
- I look forward to prospecting every day!
- I'm pleasantly persistent with every objection I receive.
- I quickly bounce back from each "no" I hear.
- I'm a great listener and don't interrupt my prospects.
- I focus on activity—not results.
- I am making 100 calls a day.

Affirmations work best when they use powerful words and are written in first person and present tense. Read your affirmations daily. Write 10 of your own affirmations—the more personal, the better.

Visualization

When you choose cold-calling as one of your top prospecting arms you also choose one of the toughest ways to prospect, so you must be ready. You will be yelled at, you will be hung up on, and you will feel like quitting. This is why this piece is important to your success. You have to prepare your mind. Visualizing is the last piece of the puzzle for your pre-prospecting routine checklist. Concentrating on the specifics of each action that must be taken to make an appointment (or whatever your goal is) is the goal here.

To get started, close your eyes, take a few deep breaths, and begin visualizing a cold call where you nail your script and deal with every objection. See yourself making a listing appointment and giving a persuasive listing presentation. Imagine the procedure for putting a house on the market and receiving an offer. Finally, picture yourself concluding the deal by receiving your commission check on the deal.

It typically takes 66 days to fully adopt a new routine. Therefore, include this pre-prospecting routine in your daily schedule. Make a commitment to following this process before beginning each prospecting session to drastically improve your outlook and meet your prospecting goals.

How to Start Prospecting?

You've done your pre-prospecting routine, and now you're ready to sit down and start making calls.

There are four things to keep in mind.

What Is Your USP, or What Do You Offer Clients?

A unique selling proposition (USP) defines your business's unique position in the marketplace, getting at the heart of your business: the value you offer and the problem you solve. A compelling USP clearly states a distinct advantage that sets you apart from your competitors.

Do you offer a special way of selling homes?

A 30-day guarantee to sell the home?

Do you offer staging?

Are you specializing in a specific area?

Do you give back to the community for every sale?

What makes you different?

Know your follow-up process. Ensure that you have your follow-up system and tools in place before you start. Do you have drip campaigns ready to go? When will you follow up? Remember to ask for referrals every so often. Always keep the lines of communication open.

Where Should You Look for Information?

REDX is what we use to get names and phone numbers. We get the information in the morning, and we start calling right away. There are many companies to choose from for data when it comes to calling a neighborhood, expired homes that were for sale, for sale by owners, and even notice of defaults. We use REDX, and you can find more information about them on our website, www.RealEstateProspecting.net, so you can get a deal from them should you choose to check it out.

The tech you use to make calls matters. The more information you have when you're calling, the better. One of the things I need when making these types of calls is accurate data and details about the current housing market so I can share that with the person I'm calling.

How Do You Keep Track?

How many calls did we make? How many were picked up? How many actual conversations were had? We use a CRM specifically for FSBOS and expired, and that's REDX. You want to keep up with your conversion rates. Or to see how to improve your process and what step you may be missing so you can get better at it. You don't know unless you track.

You can also choose to keep track of them on Trello, or a CRM such as Follow Up Boss or Chime. When I was calling expireds daily I was using Trello to do it, and I have a video on how I was doing that, which you can watch on RealEstateProspecting .net.

When you are spread out you will lose track of who you are calling if you don't keep that information somewhere. The key for me was not spreading out too much. I decided to eventually focus on two cities only, but when I first started, I was spread out between two counties: Ventura and Los Angeles County. That was a huge mistake for me because it spread me out dramatically.

Learn from my mistakes and start super small.

What Types of Leads to Call?

Expireds: Properties that were on the market but didn't sell before the listing's expiration date are known as

expired listings. Agents can obtain expired listing leads by searching for them in the MLS system or purchasing leads from a site such as REDX. For agents looking to tap into this as a specific market or secondary market to increase sales, expired listings are a great source of leads.

FSBOs: For those new agents, FSBO stands for "For Sale By Owner." They are homeowners who are trying to sell their home by themselves. They don't have agent representation. Building trust with a potential FSBO requires skill and a great prospecting strategy. As a result, you can turn FSBO leads into one of your biggest sources of clients as a real estate agent.

Demonstrating your ability to solve problems is the best way to convince an FSBO listing to become your listing. Both those looking to buy a home and those looking to sell their property can benefit from your services, resources, and marketing techniques. When it comes to FSBOs, your goal isn't so much to criticize their efforts as it is to highlight the stark contrast between your level of systems and theirs.

Just Listed/Just Sold: Any properties that you have just listed or just sold. Check with your broker, but if you're a new agent and don't have any listings or sales, you can use the brokerage's listings (since in most states the listings belong to the brokerage, not the agent).

Circle Dialing (Circle Prospecting): Circle prospecting is where you contact all homeowners surrounding a specific new listing (or just sold). The goal of circle prospecting is to generate leads by showing social proof of the listing.

For Rent By Owners (FRBO): This is an investor that has a rental property. While they may not be in the market to sell right now, they may be looking to buy more property. This type of owner is not usually married to one real estate agent, either. If you continually give them value, you can make them a client for life. This is a great all-around lead source.

Notice of Defaults (NOD): A notice of default is a public notice that a borrower is behind on their mortgage payments. (Also known as being in default on their loan.) It's typically filed with a court and regarded as the first step in the foreclosure process. NODs are an overlooked lead source because most agents don't want to spend the time combing through their local county website to find them. But they can be lucrative, especially in a down market.

Sample Scripts

Out of all the cold-calling we have done the one that seems to be the easiest to start with to get you going is circle prospecting. You can skip down to that one and try it first if you want to give a shot.

You can visit RealEstateProspecting.net to get access to my personal scripts that I use when prospecting. I'll share with you a sample of those scripts below.

Just Expired Scripts

When calling expireds, the tonality must be right. It can't be aggressive or forceful, and it has to be natural and genuine. Before you begin your calls, get yourself into the right mindset. Think of ways you can help the people who you are calling and make sure to listen. Come from contribution.

The scripts below are interchangeable and are here to help as a guide. You can modify and adjust as you see fit.

Just Expired

You: Hi _____?

Client: Yes?

You: Hi _____. This is Tristan with Happy Realty here in _____. How are you today?

Client: Good. How can I help you?

You: Great. Well, your home just came off the market. What happened?

Client: It didn't sell, that's what happened. I don't have time for this call.

You: I'm sorry about that. I'm just trying to help by seeing what you think went wrong because hundreds of homes sold all around us while yours didn't. What happened?

(Watch your tonality, *because if this is said aggressively, it can be offensive.)*

Client: The market sucks, but how did you get my number?

You: It's a service that provides your phone number and also lets us know that your home didn't sell. You're going to get a lot more calls from agents. Would you like me to take you off our list at least?

Client: Yes, please. This is Terrible.

You: Yeah, it can be overwhelming. Sorry about that. I'll remove you off our list, and I'll email my office to let them know not to call you, just in case someone at the office was also going to call you. Are you still thinking of selling this year?

(The idea behind this is a pattern interrupt. All agents are calling and asking the same questions, and you don't want to be like the other agents. You want to help, and by providing them with a partial solution you are then able to ask the question, "Are you thinking of selling this year?" or "Are you thinking of selling next year?" and they will answer it because you have their ear now.)

Client: The market wasn't great, but our real estate agent did a great job.

You: Yeah, I hear that sometimes, but it also has to do with marketing, because there are other homes that sold while yours didn't. Why do you think that is?

Client: I don't know, you're the expert.

You: Got it. Well, just by looking at your home online I can already see that we could do two things differently that could make the difference for it to sell. Do you have some time for me to stop by today at 6 p.m. or do you have time to do a video conference call so I can show you what I do that's different?

Client: No, I can't do 6 p.m.

You: OK, what time do you have today?

The key here is to go for the appointment to meet them in person or to do a presentation through Zoom or Google. It won't always work; sometimes they will shut you down here. Instead of pressing too much and losing them completely, be sure to end the conversation kindly and respectfully and then follow up with them in a few days over the phone or in person.

We Are Using the Same Agent (Objection Handler Script)

1. Got it. Your agent put in a lot of work the last time around, but (client's first name), while your home was marketed and didn't sell, others were marketed and sold. What's going to be done differently to make sure your home sells this time?

2. OK. I actually took some time to create a short list of what I would do differently if I were to market your home so that it does sell. Has your agent given you a sheet on what they will do differently this time around?

We Are Selling It Ourselves (Objection Handler Script)

You: Are you doing it to save on the commission, or for a different reason?

Client: To save on the commission. It's a few thousand dollars that we can use to buy furniture.

You: Hmmm. Do you have another three minutes for me to go over how I can sell your home for more and net you more money than doing it on your own?

Client: Yes, I've got three minutes.

You: Great! One stat comes to mind from the National Association of Realtors: the average owners sold their home for 200K, and the average for an agent-assisted sold home was $265,500.

Here's why. The difference is because a professional agent works with buyers that are ready to buy, that have been preapproved, and won't waste your time. When your home is up for sale

153

Cold-Calling

"by owner," it screams "discount" to all of the investors and bargain hunters.

The last thing you want to do is discount your home to the consumer, right?

Client: True, I don't want that, but I'm just going to put it up for sale for a little bit under what others have sold so that mine can sell quicker and I can save on the commission.

You: So why would buyers that are working with agents come to see your home if they're not going to get paid? Are you still going to offer those agents a 2.5% commission?

Client: Yes, if you bring a buyer, I'll pay that commission. You still get paid.

You: OK. I see. Let me explain it in a different way. I had a client that I was helping on the buy side. He found a home that was sold "by owner." My buyer immediately thought, "Wow, we can get that for less, because the seller doesn't know what he's doing." At that point I worked for my buyer, so I negotiated with the owner three times and got the price 10% under market value. I negotiated the first time on the purchase price, a second time on the items that needed fixing, and a third time when the seller filled out a portion of the contract incorrectly. Not only did the seller have to pay me the 2.5% commission, they also lost out 10% more because they had no representation, they had no one guiding them or watching out for them.

That's the world we live in. Not only can I save you money, but I will net you more money with the marketing that we do through specific targeting of people that like your home.

Let's meet up later today if you can?

Client: I'm not sure I'm quite ready.

You: It only takes about 25 minutes to show you. I can do it on my way back home from the office at 6 p.m. or is 7 p.m. OK? Or would you like to do a video conferencing call where we can share my screen and I can show you there?

We Aren't Going to Relist Now (Objection Handler Script)

First case:

You: OK. Are you thinking maybe at the end of this year or next year? I don't want to be calling and bothering you if you're not interested yet.

Client: Next year.

You: Thank you. I'll be in touch, and if I come across anyone that is interested in your home in the meantime, would it be OK to call you if they are super serious?

Client: Yes, but it would depend on what you mean by serious.

You: I mean, if they are ready to place an offer after they see the home from the inside. There are times that I come across those, so I just want to make sure you want me to place you on that list. It's what I call my *off market* list. I save it for serious buyers.

Second case:

You: Thank you. Would you consider it spamming if I kept you updated by email when your home price goes up or down?

Client: No.

You: Great. I'm just making sure. What's the best email to send the updates to?

Client: ****@gmail.com.

You: OK. What price do you think you would need to be at to make that move?

Client: Well, if we got to $*****, I would consider it.

You: I'll keep you updated. (You can interchange the Old Expired Script about the investors here.)

Old Expired Scripts

A great way to find gold nugget listings that didn't sell during a bear market is to call "old" expireds. I've discovered a few new listings by contacting old expired listings that weren't aware the market was improving and they had a better chance of selling now.

When calling expireds the tonality has to be right. It can't be aggressive or forceful, and it has to be natural and genuine. Before you begin your calls, get yourself into the right mindset. Think of ways you can help the people that you are calling and make sure to listen.

The scripts below are interchangeable and are here to help as a guide. You can modify and adjust as you see fit.

You: "Hello, _____?

Hi _____, this is Tristan with Happy Realty, and I'm calling about the house you were selling on _____ St. way back in 2019. Did you ever sell that home?

Client: No, we decided to stay. It was a bad time to sell at that time.

You: A lot of people didn't. Have you thought about selling your home now, in this current market?

Client: Not anymore, but thanks for calling. I'm busy right now.

You: OK. Well, thanks for your time, (first name). One last question for you. If I could get you a cash offer from one of our investors in two days, would that interest you?

Client: Depends what the offer would be.

You: Well, I work with a group of investors that are always looking to buy homes at the right price and turn around and sell them or keep them as rentals. Have you given a thought to what you would want to sell your home for?

Client: Yes, we've thought about $*****.

You: OK. I'll check to see how that matches up with what they are looking for. The market is much better than when you were trying to sell, so that may be possible. What do you think stopped your home from selling last time?

Client: The market.

You: Got it! My investors are looking for deals, so if their number doesn't match up with what you are looking for, I will let you know. Do you want me to also pull up a market analysis on your home so you know what it's worth in an open market?

Client: Sure, it won't hurt. Thanks.

You: Great. I will do that and also make a net sheet for you to show you how much you will net if you sell it for the amount you want and the amount the investor offers if it's different than your offer. I'll also make a third net sheet that shows what you would net in the open market.

Client: Great. Thank you.

You: I'll get those three estimates to you and let you know what that looks like. Can I stop by on Tuesday at 6 p.m. to drop those off and go over the net sheets with you?

Client: I have to check to make sure. Let's pencil that in.

You: It only takes about 25 minutes to show you. I can do it on my way back home from the office at 6 p.m., or is 7 p.m. OK?

Or would you like to do a video conferencing call where we can share my screen and I can show you there?

FSBO Dialogue Scripts

For Sale By Owner scripts for you to master.

You: Hi, is this the owner of the FSBO?

Client: Yes.

You: Hi, this is _____ with Happy Realty. How are you today?

Client: I'm good. You're calling about the property?

You: Great, I'm calling about the home for sale on _____. Is it still available?

Client: Yes.

You: Excellent, I have a few buyers in your area and I was wondering if you have a:

1. Formal dining room?

2. Guest house or separate sleeping quarters? (Luxury)

3. Pet policy in your HOA?

(This is a pattern interrupt. Most agents call about the home and then go right into selling their service and how amazing they are. The approach here is different and meant to interrupt the seller and have them think, so they can open up about what they really want to do with their home. When you take time to ask about something specific like a pet policy for the HOA or a formal dining room, it confirms to the seller that you have someone interested in a home similar to theirs.)

Client: Well, what do you mean by a formal dining room? I have a place for a dining table.

You: Like a separate room with a wall separating the dining room from the living room and the kitchen.

Client: No, there is no separate dining room. Sorry.

You: That's OK, it can still work. Can you tell me a little more about your home?

Client: Yes, a lot of the information is online, but the home has recently been remodeled, new roof, etc.

You: How long have you had it for sale as For Sale By Owner?

Client: Two weeks.

You:	How is it going so far?
Client:	Not bad, had a few showings. People seem interested.
You:	Did you choose to sell it on your own to save on commission or because you hate all real estate agents? Hahaha.
Client:	Both. Hahaha.
You:	Hahaha, got it. OK, so how long will you try to sell it on your own before you might look at an agent for help?
Client:	Probably two months.
You:	Hmmm. Do you have another three minutes for me to go over how I can sell your home for more and net you more money than doing it on your own?
Client:	Yes, I've got three minutes.
You:	Great! One stat comes to mind from the National Association of Realtors: the average owners sold their home for 200K, and the average for an agent-assisted sold home was $265,500.
	Here's why. The difference is because a professional agent works with buyers that are ready to buy, that have been preapproved, and won't waste your time. When your home is up for sale "by owner," it screams "discount" to all of the investors and bargain hunters.
	The last thing you want to do is discount your home to the consumer, right?
Client:	True, I don't want that, but I'm just going to put it up for sale for a little bit under what others have sold so that mine can sell quicker and I can save on the commission.

You:	So why would buyers that are working with agents come to see your home if they're not going to get paid? Are you still going to offer those agents a 2.5% commission?
Client:	Yes, if you bring a buyer, I'll pay that commission. You still get paid.
You:	OK. I see. Let me explain it in a different way. I had a client that I was helping on the buy side. He found a home that was sold by owner. My buyer immediately thought, "Wow, we can get that for less, because the seller doesn't know what he's doing."
	At that point I work for my buyer so I negotiated with the owner three times and got the price 10% under market value. I negotiated the first time on the purchase price, a second time on the items that needed fixing, and a third time when the seller filled out a portion of the contract incorrectly. Not only did the seller have to pay me the 2.5% commission, they also lost out 10% more because they had no representation, they had no one guiding them or watching out for them.
	That's the world we live in. Not only can I save you money, but I will net you more money with the marketing that we do through specific targeting of people that like your home.
	Let's meet up later today, if you can?
Client:	I'm not sure I'm quite ready.
You:	It only takes about 25 minutes to show you. I can do it on my way back home from the office at 6 p.m., or is 7 p.m. OK?

161

Cold-Calling

Or would you like to do a video conferencing call where we can share my screen and I can show you there?

Giving Value So You Can Follow Up Later Script

First option:

You: Has a realtor already sent you some items to make your sale more successful?

Client: I've gotten some things from online.

You: Well, there are a few sheets of paperwork that we have to help For Sale By Owners succeed with the sale of your home. Let me send that to you and let me know if it's helpful after you've used it.

Obviously this is in hope that if you don't end up selling on your own, you will use us to help in the future.

When is a good time for me to stop by and take a look at your home and give you the paperwork?

Second option:

You: I know you've probably heard agents tell you that they will post your listing on 300 websites and they'll post it on Facebook and Instagram and all this stuff, but has anyone sent you a video showing you how to do it on your own?

Client: No.

You: OK, I will send you one video that shows you how to create lead ads on Facebook so that you can get information from people that may be interested in seeing your home in person. What's your email?

Client:	*****@gmail.com.
You:	I'll see if I can find a company that also does a single property website so you can have a nice site that people can visit.
	The idea behind this approach is to give back to the seller and come from a point of giving value and following up every three or four days. FSBOs will most likely list quickly if they don't end up selling on their own. They are already motivated because they have their home for sale.

Circle Prospecting Dialogue

You:	Hi (first name)?
Client:	Yes.
You:	Hi (first name), this is Tristan with Happy Realty. How are you?
Client:	Great. How can I help you?
You:	I'm calling because I'm working with some buyers who are looking to move to your neighborhood. So I promised my buyers I'd call around to the neighborhood. Do you have any friends in the neighborhood who have thought about moving, that don't have their homes for sale yet?
Client:	No, don't talk to anyone here. Thanks for calling though.

You:	OK. Thanks, (first name). I appreciate your time. One last question. Have you given any thoughts about selling and moving to a different area?
Client:	No. I'm going to die here. They're going to bury me here. Hahaha.
You:	Hahaha. Thank you for taking the time to think about that. So investing in real estate is probably out of the question too, or have you thought of doing that?
Client:	We've thought about it, but everything is so expensive here.
You:	Yeah, everything is pricey. What about out of state?

If they want to invest out of state, you can refer them out to an agent. Visit the Lab Coat Agents Referral Facebook group and post the referral there. If they sound interested in possibly selling, then stay on top of them. You can nurture them if they sound like they're a possible future sale. Feel free to use some of the other scripts that can help with the closing if you need to.

Tech

REDX

RealEstateProspecting.net

Mojo

Trello

Follow Up Boss

Chime CRM

Google Sheets

Google Docs

iPhone (to record yourself talking)

Chapter 14

Networking

Real estate is a relationship business, it always has been, and it will always be. Technology and software are here to enhance those relationships if we know how to use them. Regardless of the latest and greatest gadget, it's about rubbing elbows, either in person or virtually, with other business owners. Building strong relationships is, after all, the foundation of the real estate industry. Your efforts to generate leads can be greatly influenced by including networking in your business strategy.

If you're looking to build a real network that brings in more leads and supports the growth of your business, where should you start? We have some great options:

Become Invested in Your Community

You can make invaluable connections for future business and referrals by volunteering for a cause you care about. You'll get a chance to meet locals, network, and give back all at once. Consider volunteering at an animal shelter, reaching out to your community's schools to see how you can help, or supporting a charitable walk or run. If you want to keep your volunteer work in the real estate industry, consider helping at your neighborhood Habitat for Humanity chapter or getting in touch with a local organization that promotes affordable housing. Post photos of your volunteer activities on your company's social media accounts to increase your online visibility. The charity of your choice will benefit from some exposure as a result.

Other things to consider within your community:

- Develop partnerships with local businesses. Join community boards or networking groups whose activities interest and inspire you.

- Think about collaborating with nearby schools; Career Days are a fun way to generate leads for real estate. Reach out to any nearby colleges or universities that might offer real estate courses and offer to be a guest speaker. If your brokerage is amenable, bring up the possibility of launching an internship program.

- Sponsor neighborhood events, local festivals, Little League teams, or after-school activities. When you sign up as a community sponsor, you frequently get the chance to have your company's logo printed on materials such as t-shirts, program pamphlets, or flyers. This is excellent for business branding and recognition.

- Contact the radio station in your area. Public radio programs always need content. You might be able to assist them by contributing to a show or podcast segment.

Attend Real Estate Conferences and Events

A great way to expand your connections and business is by networking at a real estate conference. Events are a great way to get referrals in addition to being a chance to improve your skills and learn about the most recent market information. Spending time interacting with individuals who might be your competition for leads may seem counterproductive, but the opposite is actually true. Real estate agents frequently focus on serving clients who are buying or selling within a particular locale or market. This means that there is a good chance that an agent you meet at an event will refer you if they come across a lead who wants something that is outside of their specialty or area of expertise.

Online Communities

My journey with this started with a real estate conference that never ended. When I was speaking around the nation for Realtor.com my wife had a crazy idea to start a Facebook group, which then became the largest community on the planet for real estate agents. It includes all social media, newsletter, events, blogs, websites, podcasts—even a Discord server.

Think about an online community for you and the people you want to attract. It could be one like my friend and coaching client from Phoenix has, "Living North Phoenix." Blair Ballin created a Facebook group that has grown to thousands of people and yes, he gets business from it.

Or think of a newsletter in the same way my friend from Fresno, California, created a newsletter called "FresYes" and made a blog out of it as well. Check out his site FresYes.com. He has over 80,000 people in his newsletter that brings valuable local information to the people who receive it. He uses Mailchimp as his newsletter builder.

Regardless of what you do make sure you start in a niche and expand from there. We tend to want to tackle something big and never break it down into a small enough segment to allow that one thing to grow first. When it comes to an online community you can even do TikTok. I have a real estate friend named Zachary Foust who has over one million followers on TikTok and has created a community there.

Some questions to ask yourself: What will your outlet be? What is your message? How often will you deliver it? Who will help you grow it?

Join the Local Chamber of Commerce

A great place to find business contacts in your area is the local chamber of commerce.

Try to regularly attend their events. Even if there is a registration fee, it is a small cost to pay considering the number of networking opportunities it will provide. Some brokerages will pay for the entire company to join, so check with your broker or team leader. Either way, it's a good investment in your business.

Don't stop there; think about contributing your time and money to chamber sponsored events. This will show locals that you are a dedicated member of the community.

Once you have a small group that consistently meets, don't be scared to also add an online component to it, like a small Facebook group.

Master the Art of the Follow Up

Networking doesn't end after you've said goodbye. Following up after a first networking introduction can be just as crucial as networking itself.

Make an effort to follow up with your previous conversation after the initial meeting. Even though you don't have to send an email before you return to your car, you should let them know how much you value their time while they are still thinking of you.

The bottom line is to network frequently and make it a habit to quickly follow up with anyone you meet.

This is why I love having a social media or online component to networking. You can stay in touch through the different content you create.

Networking Event Checklist

Before the Event

- Get in the right frame of mind with the goal of meeting people and having interesting conversations (try not to focus on selling real estate).

- Don't expect to try to gain business from the event. Instead, concentrate on building rapport with everyone you meet.

- If you are shy or anxious when speaking to strangers, wear something that will spark a conversation. These could be interesting shoes, a cute tie, or a nametag. One agent I know wears his nametag upside down on purpose so people will comment on it. It's a great conversation starter for him.

- Be ready for an answer when asked, "How's the market in your area?"

During the Event

- Remember to smile! Having confidence goes a long way.

- "Hi, I'm Tristan," is the best conversation starter ever. (Obviously use your name.)

- Remember FORD = Ask people about family, occupation, recreation, and dreams.

- Look for connections. Hobbies, interests, the location, etc.

- Make an introduction to the host. They will likely introduce you to someone else.

- When speaking, use hand gestures. Match body language with whoever you are speaking with. It will relax the other person, and they will open up to you.

- Look for wallflowers. They may just be shy and nervous as you may be.

- Stay close to the bar. People who have just had a drink are eager to socialize.

- During a conversation, avoid letting your eyes wander. Just concentrate on the person you are talking to.

- Simply putting out your hand and saying, "Well, it was great meeting you" is the best way to end a conversation.

After the Event

- Take the time to build a connection. Trust the process.

- Follow up with everyone within 24 hours. A handwritten note is a nice touch.

- Do not insist on scheduling another meeting or other business-related activity. Simply let them know how much you enjoyed meeting them.

- Make plans for your next event! Meeting people repeatedly is the key to establishing long-lasting relationships.

Online Communities Checklist

Here are some things to think about when it comes to building out communities for your business. I want you to think of this as part of your business and an actual part of prospecting. Here is how you break it down, so you get started with a Facebook group, a newsletter, a Discord server, or anything on social media.

I would be running the group, identifying the moderators, and directing the podcast and website.

1. Define your community:

    a. Find something that you can get behind, whether it's a community, a sport, something you collect, or anything that people can enjoy talking about that you love.

2. Brand your community:

    a. If you don't have one in-house graphic designer, look for one in Fiverr or 99designs and go with the logo that people would wear on a hat or T-shirt.

    b. Think of what I did with Lab Coat Agents and A Brilliant Tribe. Think of what Blair did with "Living North Phoenix" or even what Jason Ferris did with "FresYes."

3. Your cadence:

    a. This is how often will you be delivering your message. Social media will be daily and newsletter will be weekly or monthly. Make sure you create a good calendar for yourself.

4. Build a team:

   a. You can't do this alone if you want to scale this, so start looking at people you can bring in who can help you out. They can help you out by creating content and making sure you are on track with your vision.

   b. Find those people who love your content and ask if they want to contribute or help. This will start creating a stronger culture around the community.

Tech
Follow Up Boss
Discord
Facebook
TikTok
MailChimp (Newsletters)
Wordpress (Blogsite)
Fiver
99Designs
ABrilliantTribe
LabCoatAgents
FresYes
LivingNorthPhoenix

Part III

Conclusion

Chapter 15

Your Priorities

Your life shouldn't just be your business. Your life should be a harmony between self, family, and business. It's not a balance; rather, it's a rhythm that shifts daily, and the amount of time you devote to each change as you go through life.

Let's get into more detail about this, but first, a tale that most of you will find familiar.

The Fight of Two Wolves within You, Me, and All of Us

An old Cherokee is teaching his grandson about life:

> *"A fight is going on inside me," he said to the boy.*
>
> *"It is a terrible fight and it is between two wolves. One is evil—he is anger, envy, sorrow, regret, greed, arrogance, self-pity, guilt, resentment, inferiority, lies, false pride, superiority, and ego."*
>
> *He continued, "The other is good—he is joy, peace, love, hope, serenity, humility, kindness, benevolence, empathy,*

generosity, truth, compassion, and faith. The same fight is
going on inside you—and inside every other person, too."

The grandson thought about it for a minute and then
asked his grandfather: "Which wolf will win?"

The old Cherokee simply replied, "The one you feed."

I first heard the aforementioned tale when I was in my early 20s. For you to better understand what we are going to discuss, I wanted to begin the chapter with this tale.

Whatever you focus on expands. And frequently, we are concentrating on our own problems because they are what are in front of us. I want to challenge you to start focusing on priorities. Things that will help you move past your current issues.

These are the things that will elevate you to where you want to go because we all have set goals that a lot of us never achieve because we never break them down into actionable steps.

It's scientific, and many of you have heard of the reticular activating system. In essence it's your brain's filtering system. Every day it filters the thousands of thoughts you have with what it thinks is important to you. What you put in front of yourself consistently is what you will think of the most.

When it comes to our priorities and our actions, where do we begin? When it comes to figuring out what is most important to us, where do we begin? I'd like to tell you that the answer lies in the process that I've created here for you so that you can better understand where to begin. And for me, visualization was the catalyst for the entire concept.

The ability to visualize helped me think, "Let's go a little further." and "What matters the most to me?" So when I close my eyes, I would think, "OK, let's figure this out. I've done this before." But figuring out those priorities is essential. And when I'm visualizing, there are really three things that I need to go over and focus on:

Self

Family

Business

And I circulate those things through my head. What does self look like? When I'm thinking about self, what is it? Spiritual, physical, mental, and emotional. If you think of the story back to the two wolves—which one are you feeding?

Do you even take time to identify what's important to you when it comes to the self? Therefore, I've broken it down into that and family. It could also be friends, siblings, parents, grandparents. It could be whatever you want it to be when it comes to the word "family." Whoever is important in your life. Do we put any emphasis on growing those relationships that are supposed to be important to us?

When it comes to the business category, it could be your profession, your job, a start-up, or a side hustle. Whatever that is to you. The idea is to identify these and place them into something so they're clear for you.

To help with this, I created a worksheet, and I'll share it with you here:

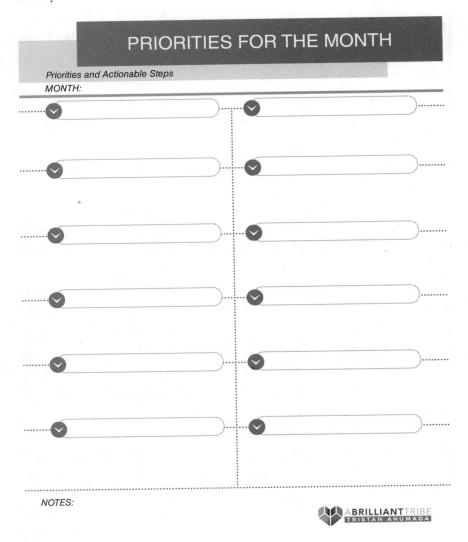

This is the actual sheet that I use. At the end of each month, I review it. It's part of the process—the month's top priorities. I list the priority by the blue check. This is the underlying principle. Knowing your priorities—self, family, and business—based on what is important to you. Then you write down the actionable steps under the priority.

I can categorize them and say that this is what I'm going to concentrate on for the month. We never take the time to decide what our priorities are, so we just let the week, the day, the month go by and react to everything that happens. The challenge lies in the fact that bad things will inevitably happen to you. After being distracted from what you had planned to do today, you return to what is most crucial.

Let's look at some examples of what I wrote.

Looking at the priority "spouse," my priority for the month is connecting with my spouse. My number one priority for that actionable step is to add it to my calendar. Because if it doesn't exist on my schedule, it doesn't exist at all.

Next, be specific. What the hell are you going to do?

When you put this on your schedule, is it just going to be on your schedule? What does that mean exactly? It means you are going to need to have clarity. Are you going to read a book? Go walking? Watch a show? Is it going to be a meeting for coffee and talking?

Then transition correctly. This is very important to me because you need to mentally prepare yourself to be with your spouse after work when you're transitioning over.

OK, I've finished what I was doing. Now I need to be present for this person. And this is who I need to be at the moment. I won't stress about anything else. This is what I need to do now. And we can apply that to everything, right? You are going to show up to work. You're going to show up at a meeting. Whatever it is that you are going to do, take the time to fully transition and be present while doing what you're going to do.

No one needs 40% of you when you can give almost 100% of yourself to each thing you are doing.

So next, I read two books a month. Under that priority is to block time. Are you a morning reader? Middle of the day, evening, when? I love reading in the evening. For me, I block my reading time for evenings.

Next is what book are you going to read? It's not just going to say, "Read a book." Be very specific about what kind of book you are going to read. Clarity gives you that extra step to accomplish that, right? So, what is it going to be?

Dividing pages needed is the third actionable step. Figure out how many pages a day you are going to read. If I need to finish this book in 2.5 weeks, this is what I need to read daily.

Once you start doing this, it becomes a little clearer.

Then I take this a step further. I will create a blueprint for the things that are going to be my priorities for the month.

This will be discussed in the next chapter.

By speaking with high achievers and business owners, I've learned that everything you undertake needs to be divided into manageable steps. In this section, I'll demonstrate how to do this using a process I've dubbed "The Process."

These are the things that will be my priorities for the month. I will make a blueprint out of them, continuing from the previous chapter when we discussed our priorities. (If you haven't read this chapter yet, please do so first.)

Professional and collegiate elite athletes increasingly adhere to a philosophy known as "the process." It is a philosophy that Alabama coach Nick Saban developed, and it states that the process of living is putting together the right actions in the right order, one after another. As a result, you work on it and then leave the process to continue.

It also enables you to shift your attention from all your issues to all your goals, viewing them as insurmountable challenges that you'll never overcome and break it into the new action steps you're developing.

So let's just focus on the one priority from the previous chapter regarding the spouse. The first step is to add this to my calendar and connect with my spouse. I am going to be very specific about what we are going to do. I have that scheduled for that day. I will briefly summarize it for the next week or two. Be very specific as to what I'm going to do at that time. I'll make sure to fully transition so that I can be present.

The key is always to break things down into small action steps so they fit in with your weekly calendar; this is the way you chip away at your big goals.

What Is "The Process"?

A few years ago, I developed this specifically for myself, but I soon realized that the method I had devised would apply to all the businesses I assist.

How This Works

You decide which of your priorities to start with. This way, you'll understand what the next steps are and why they're important to you. What problem are you solving? What are the action steps that you need to take on a daily basis? Or on a weekly basis?

First check off what type of priority it is: physical, intellectual, spiritual, business, parental, social, financial, emotional, or marital/partnership.

For this specific example, we are still focusing on the priority spouse from the last chapter.

As you proceed down the list, under "Priority," you'll have something that is specific, timely, and actionable; if you've ever used SMART goals, this will be very similar to them.

I'll be very clear: I do want to improve at being a better spouse because, well, let's just say that I can always improve. My spouse and I need to communicate more. I'm going to schedule time specifically so that I can talk to my spouse more often. Let's say it's just going to be an hour from 6 to 7 p.m.—where I can focus on my spouse. And when I describe what I'm going to do there, I'll be very detailed. That's my number one goal.

Then why is this important to me? If you are married or have a partner, you understand the value of spending time with them. In either case, I always look for the "why" behind everything we do. When I launch a new business, guess what happens when things get tough if I'm not passionate enough or if my *why* is not strong enough? I end up bailing because my passion isn't there.

Write everything out. Don't accept the first response you hear. You've got to dig deep into this. Does it make you feel significant? Do you cherish that relationship? What is so important about connecting with this other person in your life? What are the key motivators?

What problem are you solving for? That would be the next question.

The Process

It doesn't always correspond to your priorities or goals. In this case, it does. Are you feeling a disconnect with your spouse? Are you feeling like you're not as connected as you used to be?

Here's where it starts to get sticky. Now we are coming up with a strategy for our priority. The key is to have three steps to support the goal or priority that we have reviewed in the previous chapters. This is where "The Process" starts to come to life.

- Block time;
- Be specific about what we are going to do;
- Transition correctly.

Here's where it gets amazing. We started accomplishing things that you thought you could never accomplish. Because now, when you start identifying the action steps behind each one, they start going into your calendar. They start getting broken down into such small steps that it doesn't feel like it's insurmountable. You are putting this large goal that you had into mini steps. The great thing is you can apply this across your life. For your business, for your health, for your relationships!

Block Time

- What are the three action steps that I'm going to take here to block time?
- First, I'm going to add it to my calendar. Then I add the date and time.
- How often? Daily? Twice a week? Weekly? When is it? Put the details on the calendar.

This way, you're going to plan a little bit and let your spouse know.

Be Specific

- What are we going to do when it comes time? Be specific. Gather some ideas.
- Walking?
- Reading?
- Cooking together?

Now you're acting with more intention. After deciding what it is, write down a specific activity that you and your spouse or partner enjoy doing together.

Transition Correctly

- Be aware of present emotions and feelings.
- Keep that in mind as you transition. How are you showing up for the person you love or care for?
- Realize in the transition, who is this person? Who are you going to be? Are you showing up with energy? Lack of energy? Barely showing up at all? Your energy matters a lot.
- What does the transition fully look like? What are the best practices you can do instantly? Does music pump you up? What gives you energy?

Now you have the actions and can start identifying where they go in your calendar. When do you tackle these actions in your calendar?

Note: Although I don't frequently use the rewards and consequences sections, I've included them here for clients who do.

Here's another example of what it looks like if I chose three strategies that will each have three action steps that help me with the priority of connecting more with my spouse.

1. Walk with my spouse daily:

   a. 6–7 p.m. on calendar;

   b. Set alarm 20 min. prior;

   c. Walk the neighborhood (if too cold, then jump on treadmill and/stationary bike).

2. Texting:

   a. Text her funny gifs daily;

   b. Text her when I'm thinking of her throughout the day;

   c. Send pics from work to make her feel like I'm thinking of her.

3. The weekend:

   a. Set time on calendar to spend with family Saturday 7–11 a.m.;

   b. Decide what we will do ahead of time, so we do it (by Thursday of that week);

   c. Let spouse and family know what is being done so you have accountability.

This is just a simple example of how you need to break things down to make sure that each actionable step can be achieved. Once it's done you can supplement it with a new action step if you want.

Jump on the website to see other examples of "The Process" so you can get a wide range of what this looks like in your business as well: www.RealEstateProspecting.net.

Tech
Google Calendar
iPhone (to set alarm, take pics, and send gifs)
Peloton Bike/Tread
RealEstateProspecting.net

Chapter 17

Building Your Virtual Staff

In the real estate industry, the term "VA" is frequently used. You may have heard the term as it refers to a virtual assistant. I was motivated to create a VA team after reading Tim Ferriss' book *The 4-Hour Work Week*. It really opened my eyes to new opportunities.

The book suggests that hiring a virtual assistant is the best way to break free from yourself and gain more freedom so you can live your life to the fullest rather than waiting for that elusive "someday." Instead of working 80 hours a week to make only $40,000 a year, Tim now works four hours per week and averages $40,000 per month.

Today, I have 41 VAs throughout my companies, and we are growing that number on a monthly basis. When it comes to hiring, training, and motivating a virtual team, I have a lot of experience.

Let's explore what a VA is specifically and what they can do for your real estate business.

Understanding Virtual Staff Members

As you may know, VA stands for virtual assistant. But actually, it should be "VS" because "virtual assistant" has a negative connotation in some industries. I would really rather change it to virtual staff because now it encompasses so many different things.

It's not just an assistant, it's a virtual staff member. I hired one of my first VAs over 10 years ago, and she's still with me today. However, over the last three years is when I've really started scaling my business with the help of a virtual staff.

I've outlined the key steps you should take before hiring a virtual team to support your real estate business. The steps will show you how to avoid making those mistakes along the way, where to look to find the right one, how to hire them after you do, how to properly train them, and finally, how to grow your virtual team for success.

Finding Clarity on Who You Want to Hire

You need to be clear about what you are hiring virtual staff for before putting up help wanted ads. Here are some tips you can try to help find clarity.

- List the tasks you absolutely hate doing, but they come with your job or industry you are in.
- Make a list of the tasks you enjoy and love doing—so much so that people can ask you to do them for free and you wouldn't mind it one bit.
- List all the things you need to do that make money for you, regardless of whether you like doing them or not.
- Jot down all the things you've been putting off, either because you don't have the time, or the skill, to do it but you know it is necessary to grow your business.

Once you complete these lists, you'll get a better sense of what jobs you'd want or need to hire for virtual staff.

Define Your Budget

Hiring means paying, and paying means setting aside a budget.

Who do you need on your virtual staff? How many assistants do you need?

Are you hiring them part time or giving them a full-time salary?

Maybe the job is just project-based, like an event or a big online marketing campaign, where you need an extra pair of hands.

Or is it a one-off thing, like hiring a freelancer to design a website?

Depending on the skill set and the amount of time they have to work on the job, the pay will differ. Make sure you have the budget to compensate your virtual assistants fairly.

Write a Good Job Description

The more details, the better!

Include the job summary, necessary qualifications, availability, expectations, working conditions (remote or on-site), and resume specifications.

You must understand the boundaries of this position. You benefit from your job description just as much as your new hire does. They will be aware of what is expected of them, and you will have a clear plan for everything you expect them to accomplish. Additionally, this is significant in terms of compensation.

If you need help with job descriptions we have some job descriptions you can use. Visit us at www.RealEstateProspecting .com, and I know we can help you there.

Where Do You Look for Virtual Staff Members?

There are many places you can go to look for virtual staff members. It can be something as simple as asking around for a referral, like "Do you know someone who knows how to do this and is looking for some extra cash?" Or you could visit sites such as Fiverr, Upwork, and sometimes even LinkedIn, and look for candidates that fit the bill.

Fiverr is a good place if you are looking for someone for a one-off job. Part-time freelancers live on Upwork, and you can find some on LinkedIn.

If you are looking for virtual assistants outside the US, I recommend AscentVA. This is a reliable company to go to because they train their people, interview them, and do an overall good job of outsourcing the best people in the Philippines for you. It is my go-to agency and where most of my virtual assistants are from. So if you are looking for social media managers, video editors, content creators, or executive admins, then I recommend checking them out.

Another one is PowerISA. If you're looking for an ISA (inside sales agent), I would suggest this. They outsource to Mexico and have people that speak English proficiently.

Now, if you're looking to hire within the US, I'd probably look at Indeed or WizeHire. Obviously, if you're going to hire within the US, that means you'll probably pay more. Virtually, I have a team of about nine people throughout the US, and they are all great performers who also work with my VA team overseas.

These are only some options. However, I highly recommend AscentVA as that's where I gravitate to the most. One last option that I have used in the past is OnlineJobs.ph, when I want to hire directly from the Philippines.

Filtering the Candidates

Once you put up employment ads, you'll get a lot of resumes pouring into your inbox. How do you sort through these candidates and filter out the ones worth your time?

What I personally do, aside from asking for their resume, is for them to send me an introduction video as well. This gives me a better feel for who they are as a person—the way they speak, their body language, their choice of words, and their creativity. Of course, there are some people who are great on video and others who are shy, so I don't completely judge them on that. It is just my way of getting to know them a little bit better than just on paper.

I also asked for samples of their work. Now, this one has more weight in my decision than the introduction videos. Some people do a practical test that applicants need to accomplish, so you can do that, too.

Consider doing a video interview. Body language can reveal a lot about a person's level of engagement. Create your list of questions ahead of time. Try asking them personal questions such as: What's your favorite color? What do you do in your free time? What series do you watch?

These types of questions will tell you a lot about the person that you are about to hire: the things they love, the things they aspire to do, what they do in their spare time, and what they are passionate about.

Take note because sometimes the role they are applying for isn't a perfect fit for what they are passionate about. Maybe they might be a better fit for a different role that you also need.

If you're specifically looking to hire an amazing assistant I highly recommend reading the book by Michael Hyatt *Your World-Class Assistant*.

Hire and Communicate

Once a person is now part of your team, your next step is to train them well.

For example, I just recently hired a tech director for the tech we use on the real estate side of my business. Some of those we use are Follow Up Boss, Chime, Ylopo, and some automation tech, such as Agent Legend.

For their first month, I let them focus on training with these tools. Some tech companies offer training on the back end of their systems where you can just login and it teaches you how to fully operate everything. I had previously taken the time outline for what should be worked on through Trello by making cards in each section. You can also use Trainual to record training, or you can just shoot a whole bunch of videos on your computer using Loom and upload to YouTube and share with your new hire.

Once they finish all their training, I or someone on my team will identify the holes in their knowledge and plug in those gaps. This way, I make sure everyone is up to par with my expectations and needs.

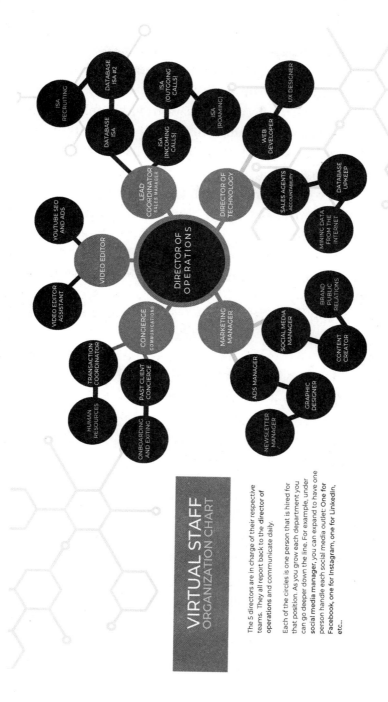

VIRTUAL STAFF
ORGANIZATION CHART

The 5 directors are in charge of their respective teams. They all report back to the director of operations and communicate daily.

Each of the circles is one person that is hired for that position. As you grow each department you can go deeper down the line. For example, under social media manager, you can expand to have one person handle each social media outlet: One for Facebook, one for Instagram, one for LinkedIn, etc...

ISA RECRUITING
DATABASE ISA #2
DATABASE ISA
ISA (OUTGOING CALLS)
ISA (ROAMING)
ISA (INCOMING CALLS)
UX DESIGNER
WEB DEVELOPER
LEAD COORDINATOR SALES MANAGER
DIRECTOR OF TECHNOLOGY
SALES AGENTS ACCOUNTABILITY
DATABASE UPKEEP
MINING DATA FROM THE INTERNET
YOUTUBE SEO AND ADS
VIDEO EDITOR
DIRECTOR OF OPERATIONS
VIDEO EDITOR ASSISTANT
CONCIERGE COMMUNICATIONS
MARKETING MANAGER
BRAND PUBLIC RELATIONS
SOCIAL MEDIA MANAGER
CONTENT CREATOR
TRANSACTION COORDINATOR
PAST CLIENT CONCIERGE
ADS MANAGER
HUMAN RESOURCES
ONBOARDING AND EXITING
GRAPHIC DESIGNER
NEWSLETTER MANAGER

195

Building Your Virtual Staff

Make sure you have an idea of where the training is coming from. You can look for a company that can provide training for you. This is consistent growth that needs to happen, and it comes in the form of training.

Another big part is communication. How are you going to communicate with these amazing people that you are hiring?

I have a rule for every single virtual assistant that joins the team. I have to communicate with them the way I communicate the quickest. Because I want them to have success, and I want to have success as well. So I require everyone to have an iPhone so we can communicate through iMessage. This way, regardless of what part of the country or world they're in, we can communicate because all we need is an email and an iPhone. We also use Google Chat in Google Spaces and have recently played around with Discord as a place to communicate daily; it's working well and it's free.

Others use Slack or similar tech. There are many modes of communication you can use, including Facebook Messenger, WhatsApp, and even Instagram Messenger. The main point is to decide how you will communicate daily with your team.

Communication, a healthy one at that, is what's going to bring the virtual team together.

Expand and Delegate

As you succeed and your business grows, your team will grow as well. When your team grows, it is important to have some sort of organizational structure just so there is a clear chain of command and accountability.

There are different ways you can organize your team, but this is the <u>virtual staff organization chart</u> I use for A Brilliant Tribe. As my team grows, this chart will also expand. Sometimes you might even have to reorganize it.

You can use that chart I created as a guide on www .RealEstateProspecting.com.

Last, I want you to start developing the mindset of *"What can I do more by delegating?"* and *"Whose skills can be better applied on the team?"*

As your business grows and you succeed, the list of things you need to do also keeps growing. If you try to do everything yourself, things will start falling through the cracks. Delegate some tasks to your excellent team members so you can do more things and focus on the important stuff that you cannot delegate to others. When you're falling behind on something, see if it's because you lack assistance in something you should be delegating or hiring out to do.

Working with a virtual staff member can help you improve the way your real estate business operates while managing your personal and professional needs. This will allow you to focus on spending more time outside of work or on growing your real estate business.

Tech
Realestateprospecting.com
AscentVA.com
Upwork.com
Fiverr.com
OnlineJobs.ph
Spaces.Google.com

Slack.com
Discord.com
PowerISA.com
Wizehire.com
Followupboss.com
Chime.me
Ylopo.com
Whatsapp.com
Facebook.com
Messenger.com
Instagram.com
Trainual.com
Loom.com
Youtube.com
AgentLegend.com
Linkedin.com

Chapter 18

Building a Real Estate Team

I frequently receive questions about the ins and outs of building a real estate team while coaching. Here, I'll give an overview of it using some factors you ought to consider before forming a real estate team. However, I want to start off by saying that I could write a whole book about forming and leading a team. As a result, this chapter merely serves as an overview of the important factors you should consider when building a team.

How Do You Know When It's Time?

One thing you'll want to consider before launching a real estate team is whether or not it's the right decision for your business. There are some things that should be considered first, such as whether you are feeling burnt out from nonstop work and whether you are running around all day, working 12- to 16-hour days.

The maximum amount an individual agent can handle alone typically ranges from 50 to 60 transactions per year, so if your average is only one every week, then maybe hiring someone else might make more sense than doing it all yourself. My breaking point was about 50 transactions as a solo agent, but even then, I had a transaction coordinator helping me manage the paperwork, and I also had a part-time assistant helping me with part of the admin work.

You also need to consider if you'll be able to bring in enough new business to get a good return on new hires. Making the decision to launch a real estate team can be exciting and even emotional, but balancing the financial realities is essential. It's important to think about where you will be creating opportunities for the agents you bring on to your team to grow. Will you give them clients to work with or will they have to find their own? Will you help coach and guide them or will they get that from your broker?

If you are a solo agent who doesn't have the systems and tools in place and isn't bringing in a lot of business, starting a team should be the last thing on your mind. You won't gain more wealth just by hiring more people. Since it will cost you more money, you should make sure that your company is profitable enough to support not only your family but also your staff.

I would start by hiring a coach to set all the right processes up to be able to succeed quicker as you start your team.

Do You Have What It Takes to Lead a Team?

Even if you're successful as a one-person band, managing a team calls for a unique set of abilities.

Many agents are unaware of the degree of change required to advance from being a top agent to a top team leader. But if you have leadership skills or are willing to acquire them, building a powerful team might be the best course of action for you.

I would suggest you look at your leadership style first. Are you a person who loves to help others grow or do you expect people that are around you to just do things without explaining to them what to do?

You will have to set a time to meet with your team weekly. My suggestion is to set time daily to talk to them for a few minutes so that everyone on your team knows what direction they are going.

You will have to set time to train your team weekly and set time to answer questions that each team member has in regards to the real estate business. Above all else you must want to help others grow by leading the way. If you want to take this on, then you will find a way to lead. There are no excuses. Your desire to move forward will be the number one reason you find a way.

Is Your House in Order?

Do you have the right systems and tools in place to have a stable foundation for your team?

Setting your revenue targets and working backward to determine how many leads and team members you'll require to meet them should be your first step when assembling a real estate team. One great system we use to track our transactions and our goals is a software company called Sisu.

As team leader, your real role is to generate leads. It's crucial that your systems can handle an increase in lead volume so your agents are ready to manage those leads from many sources.

Your key systems and tools to have in place before hiring are:

Database

Brand Kit

Referrals

Listing inventory

Transaction management

Lead generation and follow-up/conversion (including online leads)

Social media marketing

Financial reports

Coaching

Get your house in order and ready to start firing on all cylinders by heavily relying on your tech stack.

What Is Your Mindset?

I recently spoke to Leisel and Donnell Taylor, who are team leaders with Village Premier Collection DMV in Lanham, Maryland, and they agreed that mindset is one of the most important things to consider when deciding to build a team.

Leisel says to remember a few things when it comes to mindset:

1. You're going to be a servant leader, coach, mentor, boss, and sometimes a psychiatrist.
2. You must be learning based.
3. You must be the rainmaker (the one who brings in the business and the leads).
4. You must be ready to train your team members.

I asked Leisel if she ever had clients who only wanted to work with her as the team leader/rainmaker. She responded that *"clients want to work with you because of the level of service you provide them that shows you know what you're doing. If you can replicate that with your team members, then they will want to work with your team members."*

Who Will Be Your First Hire?

In Chapter 17, we discuss building a virtual staff. This is a good place to start with hiring administrators and transaction coordinators. If you haven't read that chapter yet, do that first and then come back here.

Many team leaders will rush to add a buyer agent when they start getting overwhelmed with business. This is usually not the place to start. You should have your core business systems in place before bringing in a buyer agent or even a showing assistant.

Your producing agents cannot be expected to be proficient in administration duties. That's why it's so important to get your real estate systems up and running as quickly as possible. When your powerhouse agents do join, they can then just plug in and keep working without becoming slowed down by cumbersome workflows and paperwork.

Agents who routinely close more than 25 deals annually shouldn't have a problem affording full-time administrative assistance. If you read the virtual staff chapter, then you know that there are some affordable remote options to help you if you're buried in paperwork.

When I reached 25 deals for the first time in my career, I decided to hire a transaction coordinator of my own. She was local and worked out of my office in Thousand Oaks, California. She kept all the files neat and orderly and she made sure that I didn't miss any signatures and that all the parties involved in the transaction were communicated within a timely manner.

Start with a transaction coordinator or an admin. You can then work yourself up to marketing director, tech director, and creative director, but it takes time. Now it's even easier to track paperwork with companies such as Open To Close. It's gotten more streamlined.

Buyer Agent (BA)

Besides putting some ads on Wizehire, Indeed, LinkedIn, and Social, be sure to let your manager or office broker know because they may be able to help you hire great people for your team.

Now you should be ready to hand off all—or most—of your leads to an expert buyer agent (BA). Making sure no lead falls through the cracks is this buyer agent's top priority. Your lead generation system should be up and running smoothly and ready to generate leads, follow up on those leads, and convert them. You should have drip campaigns ready. Your BA needs a ready-made, foolproof lead cultivation strategy, and you should be prepared to hold them responsible for database upkeep and follow-up.

Be sure to have them sign a contract so everything you agree to is in writing and nothing is left to chance. Chances are high that your first buyer agent will leave and you don't want it to happen without a contract in place.

A minimum of two transactions should be possible for your buyer agent each month. You build up to that slowly as you train them with the right verbiage and approach. Prepare to add your second buyer agent or an ISA (inside sales agent) when it appears that you might surpass four closings per month for each and every BA that you employ.

Inside Sales Agent (ISA)

Congratulations! Now that you have a dedicated BA, guess what you can do now. You are free to go out and get a ton of new listings. However, a word of advice: be prepared for things to become extremely busy on both sides. Your team may be tempted to focus only on the hot leads that close quickly. Remember you still have to dedicate time to nurture and cultivate the warm leads, too.

This would be the best time to hire your first inside sales agent, or ISA. A great ISA can double your GCI (gross commission income) within the first year just by simply taking over the tasks that agents don't want to do, such as making calls. Actually, that is all they should be doing is dialing all day long.

Prompt, regular follow-up is a *must*, and this results in more leads and more closed sales.

Recently I had Justin Havre, the #1 Re/Max team in Canada in closed transactions, on a webinar and we talked about his experience with hiring ISAs for his team. He shared that he offers an ISA position for someone that is getting licensed. He gives them the opportunity to get comfortable with scripts and dialogue before they become a licensed agent. He said they offer a six-month commitment at a minimum. Within that time frame he commits to training them and giving them a job while they are getting a real estate license. Justin pays them as employees.

Justin is a big proponent of investing time in training his staff and agents.

"If someone really fails, it's your responsibility," Justin says.

I couldn't agree more.

Justin is a smart person, and he's worked hard to get to where he is. You have options to hire ISAs overseas too. One of the companies we use is Power ISA, so when you're ready to get an ISA, be sure to check them out. The very first ISA I hired was a local person. He did well on the team, and in fact, I still have him on the team. He became a good friend. In the many years he's been on the team as ISA I've learned that I need to give my ISAs time to take breaks.

Building a Real Estate Team

Calling nonstop is not easy, so many breaks are required to refocus and recenter yourself. Treat your ISAs with respect and kindness, and, of course, get a contract in place. I prefer that my ISA have a real estate license, but it's not required all the time. Be sure to ask your broker and find out what your state laws require.

Listing Agent (LA)

As the team leader, it is your duty to make sure you always have listings because listings equal leads, which keeps your pipeline full.

Your ability to consistently close deals must be shown, along with maintaining team engagement. Once you've handled as many listings as you can on your own, it's time to add either a listing agent (LA) or a listing agent coordinator to accomplish this.

If you decide to go the route of an LA transaction coordinator, prepare to spend around $300–700 range per transaction. This should be completely manageable for most teams.

More Team Roles

It's time to evaluate your team and consider expanding it every time you surpass a new revenue goal.

The possibilities are endless, from showing assistants to social media directors to squad leaders. These are merely a few strategies for expanding your team. It's important to remember that your personal and professional objectives will determine exactly how your real estate team is structured, which will ultimately help you find that elusive work-life balance.

Among the most frequently cited books on the subject is without a doubt Gary Keller's *The Millionaire Real Estate Agent*. What readers value most is that the lessons can be used by teams of any size. I would suggest reading this book if you want to learn more about growing your team using the MREA model.

How to Hire Using the DISC

Strong team dynamics are crucial for team leaders, but not everyone takes the time to fully comprehend how their team works.

Knowing a candidate's personality traits and preferences can help you assess their compatibility and make it easier for you to work with the team you already have.

A personality assessment tool can provide you with a framework for comprehending the various personality types of your current or potential team members.

Actually, there are lots of ways to use DISC behavioral styles in the real estate industry. For instance, based on these styles, you might decide who to hire for a real estate team or how to train a new team member. In fact, it might even specify how you ought to proceed in a listing appointment when dealing with a specific kind of client.

The best personality assessment tool to use to determine which one is best for you is the DISC assessment.

How Does the DISC Assessment Work?

The DISC is a four-trait personality assessment tool that is the most widely used team building tool in the real estate industry. More than one million people use it every year to help them hire and train staff and employees.

The simplicity of the DISC is its greatest asset. The following characteristics are listed, and each team member is asked to rate their own propensity toward each of them:

Dominance (D): Direct, strong-willed, and forceful;

Influence (I): Sociable, talkative, and lively;

Steadiness (S): Gentle, accommodating, and soft-hearted;

Conscientiousness (C): Private, analytical, and logical.

Team members and leaders can choose how to communicate with one another based on their DISC profiles.

For instance, when you demonstrate your passion for a goal or target, a high D will be most motivated. A high C person, however, will be interested in the specifics of how and why that goal was established. Of course, it's possible for someone to be high on both D and C, in which case you should appeal to their enthusiasm as well as their love of specifics.

Overall, a real estate agent must be people-oriented, able to connect with clients right away, establish a rapport, pay attention to their wants and needs, and be relatable to them. The ideal candidate would have a strong background in customer service, excellent communication skills, and an honest demeanor.(Graphic)

What does DiSC mean?

DiSC is an acronym that stands for the four main personality profiles described in the DiSC model:
(D)dominance, (I)influence, (S)steadiness, and (C)conscientiousness.

People with D personalities **tend to be confident and place an emphasis on accomplishing bottom-line results.**

People with i personalities **tend to be more open and place an emphasis on relationships and influencing or persuading others.**

People with S personalities **tend to be dependable and place an emphasis on cooperation and sincerity.**

People with C personalities **tend to place the emphasis on quality, accuracy, expertise, and competency.**

Everything DiSC also measures priorities (the words around the circle), providing more nuanced and memorable feedback in profiles.

Go with Your Gut

With almost 20 years of experience, I consider myself an expert when it comes to selecting a team. I now take my time with hiring. Here's what my hiring process looks like:

- First, we conduct an initial phone screening.
- Next is an interview, which incorporates the DISC type tool. The main focus of this step is weeding out the candidates that may not be a good fit.
- Finally, the candidate is interviewed by the team and the team decides if they make the cut. The team must be able to get along with the person being hired.

No matter what position I'm hiring for, I always go with my gut when making a decision. In the book *Limitless* by Jim Kwik, he went over the science behind "the gut," so don't write it off just yet.

Hire Slow, Fire Slow

In the real estate industry, the advice to "hire slow, fire fast" has become a leadership mantra, but I'm telling you right now it's all wrong. Once you have your principles and values outlined it's fairly easy to hire quickly, but I still suggest you hire slowly so you don't skip a step.

Just because we fire slow doesn't mean we don't let people go if they aren't working out. The morale of the entire team can be ruined by one or two toxic individuals. The team will perform better the sooner you let them go. It makes no difference how many homes this person sells. If they aren't a team player, they gotta go.

The responsibility of a leader is to preserve the focus of their team, second only to lead generation. Getting rid of the bad apples is difficult, especially the first time, but it's necessary to prevent them from spreading their negativity to the team as a whole.

And keep in mind that the best course of action is to avoid hiring the wrong person in the first place; this is why it's so important to set your principles and values from the get-go. What I've found over the years is that there are two problems with the old mantra "Fire Fast." Number one is that you forget the reason that you hired the person in the first place. Think about why you hired them; there was a great reason, right? Well, something happened along the way, and it's important to look internally first to make sure it's not mainly your fault or your team's fault that they have failed. Number two, don't fire with your ego. Take a step back and make sure that it's not your ego getting rid of them quickly but that it's a valid reason you are letting them go.

I have people on my team that have been with me for over 13 years, and they are amazing! I had to change internally to become a better leader along the way so that they could also succeed at a higher level on the team. It's not always them; sometimes it's you.

Always Lead with Your "Why"

You've got to lead with "why" with every single decision you make for your team.

But why is **"why"** so important?

Your team is there to support your clients and expand your business while relieving some of the burden from you, the team leader. Having to micromanage defeats the purpose.

Having the right systems and tools in place and hiring the right people are undoubtedly the keys to success in this, in my experience. But none of these matters if your team isn't made up of motivated individuals who know exactly why they are a part of your team and feel compelled to support you in your efforts to accomplish more.

Knowing your employees' personalities and preferences will help you understand a lot about what drives them. You'll be successful in keeping them engaged and prepared to work each day if you align their personal drivers with the overall mission of the company.

The most effective teams share a common set of values, beliefs, and goals.

How Do I Keep My Team Motivated?

I start each week with a morning call to keep my team on task and inspired.

This is my most frequent and reliable action for maintaining team engagement. Nearly every week on Monday or Thursday at 8:30, my team and I have a chat. I select a subject for discussion, query the group, and occasionally gather feedback.

I use that time to connect and motivate my team. The morning call has brought my team closer together and has elevated our culture.

I believe that the best way to keep your staff motivated is to instill a powerful combination of gratitude and determination—each and every day.

If you really want to go deeper with your team, you have to communicate throughout the day, texting, calling, social media, and going out to coffee, pickleball, or whatever time you can to connect and talk.

The number one thing that keeps the team motivated is the one-on-one meetings I do. I pick a local coffee shop, and I meet with my team here and there individually, where I take notes and we build a plan together for them to succeed more. We talk about the struggles, we talk about the challenges, and we lay out a plan for what's next.

Be Ready to Fail Forward

Recognize that the process will be difficult and time consuming. Most likely, your initial attempt will end in failure. Don't let the fact that no one else is as devoted as you are cause you to feel inferior or to lose focus.

There is a reason you are the team leader.

Accept the fact that you will make your fair share of poor hiring decisions and learning experiences. But doing that is what improves you and makes you stronger.

And occasionally doing that is what makes it enjoyable.

Change Your Environment

It was 2004, my first year in real estate, and I was holding an open house. I took some time before the open house to drop off some black-and-white flyers around the multimillion-dollar open house. The home was listed by another agent in my office, and it wasn't mine. A few days after the open house was finished, I received a callback from a flyer I dropped off. In fact, it was a possible seller that needed to sell their $4 million house. The first thing I did was calculate the possible commission, but then I realized that I had never sold a home over one million. After that, I got as ready as I could by talking to my broker and other luxury agents in my office.

The day of the appointment I showed up all suited up. Best shoes, amazing dark gray suit, striped, purple tie, and well groomed. I toured the home, sat down in the living room and I remember two things like it was yesterday: One, I was sweating a ton! Two, my answer to their question about commission.

"So, Tristan, why are we going to pay you $125,000 in commission?" the homeowner asked me.

I took a hard swallow and answered, "Because that's the commission."

Soon after that we all got up and they kindly walked me out the door and I never heard back from them because they listed and sold the home with agents that were way more experienced than me.

When people asked me how it went, I told them that I didn't get the listing and what I kept on hearing was that I wasn't ready for that type of listing. Phrases like, "Makes sense, you need more experience" and "You can't do that your rookie year" and "It's going to take you a few years until you're able to list and sell a home like that." All of those phrases became my reality.

Building a Real Estate Team

You see, instead of asking myself questions that would allow me to rebound and succeed quickly, I replayed those lines in my head over and over. I also created some of my own stories in my head. Stories like, "You're too young to sell those types of homes" and "Maybe luxury home sales are not for you, you don't come from money, so it makes sense that you stick to lower-priced homes."

Yeah, that played in my head for years.

Until I started changing my environment, through books, people, live events, podcasts, and webinars. I started asking questions that would have me take action steps to achieving success in the real estate luxury world. It wasn't until 11 years later that I finally sold a multimillion-dollar home. You know what happened next?

I sold more and more. I started a team. I became successful.

In fact, one of our sales was for $13.1 million when our client bought Matthew Perry's (the actor from *Friends*) home in Malibu. I tell you this story only to show you that I was my own enemy. My own detriment to growth. The one thing that was stopping me was the fact that I wasn't asking myself the right questions that could develop me into a better human being, a better real estate agent, or a person that could bring value to more people. I was simply playing a story of defeat and failure over and over in my head.

To help you get started with building a team, we've included a business checklist courtesy of Leisel Taylor. This is the exact same checklist she used to help her build a powerhouse team.

Business Checklist

- Are you truly operating as a business? Create a name for your business. (Get a CPA as soon as possible and go over this list with them.)

- Create a business entity for your team. Decide whether an LLC or S Corp is the best option for you. Consult with your tax professional regarding tax advantages.

- Obtain your EIN number from the IRS—it's *free*. Apply for your EIN so that you can get paid in the name of your business to receive tax advantages.

- Open a business operating account, business savings account, and business tax account. Do not commingle your business and personal funds. Avoid tax problems.

- Decide what will be your team structure. You will need to create an organizational chart to define the roles of your team members and note who is responsible for what.

- Create your vision and mission statement. What is your purpose? What are your goals? What are you doing in the community to help others? This will be part of the culture that you create for your team and your business.

- Create a one-, three-, and five-year business plan. You must have a path to follow. Where do you see your team and business in year one? Where do you see your team growth and business in year three? Where do you see your growth in year five?

- Compile financial statements for your business and team. You should have a balance sheet and profit and loss statement to track revenue coming in and the expenses that you invest in your business. When you review your one-year, two-year, and three-year expenses, you will post areas in your spending that will need to be trimmed or other areas in which to invest more into your business because there was a great return on investment.

● Get right with the IRS. Pay estimated taxes quarterly. As a business owner, you must pay estimated taxes quarterly. These are conversations you should be having with your tax professional.

"You aren't starting a team. You are starting a business."
—Leisel Taylor

Finally, Leisel recommends playing "Red Light, Green Light" when starting out with a real estate team. Here are four things you should do.

Red Light, Green Light

1. Lead with revenue and track your expenses. Check the ROI on items that you are spending your money on before adding on additional expenses in your business. Track these items for a minimum of five months.

2. Start operating your business as a business.

3. Stay away from shiny objects. As realtors, we are guilty of chasing after the *new best* thing instead of focusing on the activities that generated business in the first place.

4. Have a budget model and a business plan to follow.

Tech
Wizehire.com
Indeed.com
LinkedIn.com
Success.com/DISC
Sisu.com
Followupboss.com
Chime.me
OpenToClose.com
PowerISA.com

Chapter 19

The Future of Real Estate

According to the National Association of REALTORS®, the number of real estate agents in the United States has increased steadily since hitting a low in the years following the 2008 mortgage meltdown, and has reached over 1.5 million at the end of 2020. I believe that the record-breaking pace of the real estate market, driven by the pandemic, has contributed to this upward trend. This suggests that many agents have never worked in a market that is "normal" and may have started their real estate careers during a time of unprecedented demand.

I work with clients who are concerned about how to succeed over the long term and how to position themselves for creating a career in this world. The same goes for seasoned agents who want to maintain their momentum through a rough patch.

These tips should help you to successfully navigate both favorable and unfavorable market conditions, enabling you to continue building a solid and reliable real estate business.

Keep Up with Trends

Real estate success frequently depends on having a keen sense of when new developments are happening and being in the right place at the right time. As a result, when you analyze both the national economy and your local market, you must keep the future in mind. Even though it might be challenging to stay current on news when you are preoccupied with serving clients, you should keep your eye on the market. That being said, also remember that real estate is regional. What is happening in California may not be what is going on in Florida. You could have a hot sellers' market in one state and see an upward swing in buyers in another. Do your own research and don't believe everything you read. Most importantly, jump into the Lab Coat Agents website and join the Facebook group so you can stay up to date with the latest practices for being a real estate agent.

Research Market Statistics

Studying the trends and statistics released by your local and state associations is one of the best ways to stay ahead of market trends. Discover the hottest neighborhoods, the most popular home styles, and the location of the upcoming business development. Utilize this knowledge to guide your marketing strategy and initiate crucial discussions with those in your sphere of influence. Keeping your SOI and past clients informed is the key to success in *any* market. It's a reason to "touch" them and also an opportunity to ask for referrals. Jump into Keeping Current Matters for national news and check out Altos Research to find localized real estate news. Both have a cost but are worth it if you want to stay informed.

Always Be Prospecting

Prospecting shouldn't be a necessity but rather a habit. You can't wait to prospect until you need business. You should always be prospecting so that there is always a steady stream of new leads in your pipeline. If you're just starting out and don't have a big budget for paid marketing, you should focus more on social media, your sphere, and professional networking. Go back and read our chapter on online marketing, farming, and networking to get an idea of what you should be doing. Remember that prospecting is not about "always closing," it's about always doing your best to create relationships.

Develop Sources for Post-Sale Referrals

Creating new leads is much more expensive than keeping an existing client satisfied. Instead of pursuing cold leads, start focusing on the people you've already worked with.

Find out about their possible present and future real estate needs by asking for testimonials and reviews. If you don't ask, you will not usually get; the idea of asking for what you want is biblical in nature. Just ask.

Make Education a Priority

Your real estate education shouldn't end once you've obtained your license or fulfilled the yearly renewal requirement. Spend some time looking for opportunities to learn about new trends and market changes in your area. Check your local or state association for webinars, online courses, and other opportunities for continuing education. Take your newly acquired knowledge even further by participating in a mastermind group or attending a conference. Remember that Lab Coat Agents has free webinar and an amazing YouTube channel that is all free for real estate agents.

Get a Coach

Everyone, regardless of profession, needs a coach. We will eventually reach a ceiling in our self-learning. It's possible that we'll experience a breakthrough in our business only to become stuck in a rut. We ask ourselves, "Where do I go from here to keep winning?" When do we need to hire a coach in order to keep growing our business?

You hire a coach when you want something to change and you are ready to learn more from someone else. If you are satisfied with your current performance or feel like you don't need one, then you don't need one.

If you need a coach, be sure to jump into www.ABrilliantTribe .com, and check out the options there. Remember that a coach is like a trainer; they are making you better as you go.

Be Open-Minded about the Next Stage of Your Career

You might have started your real estate career by focusing on FSBOs and expireds. Perhaps it's time to turn your attention to building a team or merging with a larger team or brokerage. You might have entered the market at a time when demand and home values experienced an unheard-of increase. You might work with struggling and distressed homeowners in the coming years. Making a name for yourself in social media could be your next step.

Find out what inspires you. What about real estate excites and motivates you? What is your "*why*"? Read the book *Start with Why* by Simon Sinek to dig deeper into your "why." Keep an eye out for a niche that has room for expansion and long-term appeal. A career in real estate can be started in so many different ways. Don't restrict yourself by believing that you must follow the crowd. In the years to come, change it up and discover fresh difficulties as well as opportunities.

Tech

www.KeepingCurrentMatters.com

www.AltosResearch.com

www.LabCoatAgents.com

www.ABrilliantTribe.com

Index

226

227